POETRY COM

GREAT MINDS

Your World...Your Future...YOUR WORDS

From London Vol II
Edited by Steve Twelvetree

Young**Writers**

First published in Great Britain in 2005 by:
Young Writers
Remus House
Coltsfoot Drive
Peterborough
PE2 9JX
Telephone: 01733 890066
Website: www.youngwriters.co.uk

SB ISBN 1 84602 077 8

Foreword

This year, the Young Writers' 'Great Minds' competition proudly presents a showcase of the best poetic talent selected from over 40,000 up-and-coming writers nationwide.

Young Writers was established in 1991 to promote the reading and writing of poetry within schools and to the youth of today. Our books nurture and inspire confidence in the ability of young writers and provide a snapshot of poems written in schools and at home by budding poets of the future.

The thought, effort, imagination and hard work put into each poem impressed us all and the task of selecting poems was a difficult but nevertheless enjoyable experience.

We hope you are as pleased as we are with the final selection and that you and your family continue to be entertained with *Great Minds From London Vol II* for many years to come.

Contents

Rosie Demellweek (13)   68
Aysha Nicholson (13)   69
Irene Williams (11)   69
Azmin Hussain (11)   70
Hannah Thayer (13)   71
Öznur Macit (14)   72
Abena Atta-Dankwa (14)   72
Tashika Warburton (13)   73
Fatos Evre (13)   73
Aminata Fofana (13)   74
Leyla Sokucu (11)   74
Niesha Baptiste (13)   75
Victoria Ault (12)   75
Derya Yesilyurt (11)   76
Laila Hadjimi (11)   76
Prisciela Kwatiah (13)   77
Joy Akata (13)   77
Selin Kavlak (13)   78
Amandah Simukai (13)   78
Clio Martin (13)   79
Hannah Cowley (13)   79
Natasha Gane (13)   80
Serap Gifci (14)   80
Cornelie Dipenge Mayaza (13)   81
Daze Osuide (13)   81
Sangeeta Singh (13)   82
Lucy Stephens (11)   82

St Martin-in-the-Fields High School for Girls

Belinda Sarkodie (13)   83
Isha Blake (11)   83
Alexandra Chan (13)   84
Moriam Kolapo (11)   84
Justina Smith (13)   85
Latoyah Henry (13)   85
Remi Oshibanjo   86
Monique Hector (11)   86
Bethan Chaplin Dewey (11)   87
Sapphire Johnson (13)   87
Whitney Warren (11)   88
Krista Gardier (13)   88

The Grey Coat Hospital

The Poems

The Eagle

Gliding, gliding, day by day,
Showing their colours and going astray,
Through the wind and in the clouds,
Above the fields of golden rye,
Showing their beauty in the open sky.

Their wings spread out,
Looking beautiful from their early spring moult,
Fluttering around, circling the ground,
High above in the mountains.

Landing on trees, balancing gracefully,
But when they're staying put you can appreciate
Them fully, as still as a statue,
Looking perfect and peaceful.

But where eagles should really be,
Is in their haven where they belong.
In their home in the sky,
Where eagles are truly meant to be.

Simon Duong (12)
Bacon's College

If I Were . . .

If I were the sun,
I would be bright and friendly,
I would sit in a lovely blue sky,
I would give people hope, light and warmth;
I would set in an orange sky and leave peacefully.

Alexander Man (11)
Joseph Clarke School

Summer

Summer is great and summer is hot,
The season has changed from dark to light;
Everything is quiet,
Bright in the wake of the sun.
People eating ice creams,
Girls and boys sharing money
Babies smiling and laughing.
Shadows are dark, cool in the shade under the trees,
The concrete is hard and hot.
Fruit salad with whipped cream,
Makes you feel free and royal;
Mermaids and fish swim beneath the ocean,
Dive deep, down and down.
On the seabed there are lots to explore:
Sand, shells, rocks and diamonds,
Treasures of the entire world.
The umbrella opens to spread out like a rainbow,
The whole sky of Heaven.
Millions of flowers spread out wide,
Open thin petals, palm trees shake,
Coconuts tumble down creating a big bash,
Juice bursts out!
Sounds of birds singing,
Children playing, echoing in the sky,
Spirits rejoice, flying about, spreading happiness.
Ripe fruit tastes scrumptious,
Wonderful and beautiful;
Summertime, I love it!

Helen Tran (11)
Joseph Clarke School

Babies

Big ones,
Small ones,
Fat ones,
Thin ones,
Tall ones,
Short ones,
Crying ones,
Quiet ones,
Crawling ones,
Walking ones,
Talking ones,
And even naughty ones!
But all babies are special in their own way.

Danielle Khan (11)
Joseph Clarke School

If I Were . . . Haiku

If I were a dog,
I'd be trotting round the fields,
Having lots of fun.

Umer Bhula (11)
Joseph Clarke School

Poem About Food

The beautiful aromas of herbs and spices,
A hot curry dish with green chillies and plain naan bread,
The duck sizzling in its own sauce with green peppers and onions,
Plumped duck tikka, grilled with salad and plain rice.

Shahida Begum (11)
Mulberry School for Girls

My Favourite Food

Burgers and chips are very common
Apples and strawberries can't be forgotten
I like junk food and I like fruit
But when they're together they just don't suit!

I like rice and I like chicken
I like tomatoes when I get to pick 'em!
I don't like broccoli and I don't like cabbage
But I leave them in the Sunday package!

If there's chocolate and if there's cake
Then on my birthday that's what I'll bake!

I like coffee and I like tea
I like biscuits to join with me!
I like salt and I like spice!
I would like them scattered on my rice!

Tahmina Jalal (11)
Mulberry School for Girls

Chicken, Chicken!

The delicious chicken about to roast,
Has just started to boast.
In the oven it goes,
And then starts to doze.
After it comes out,
The smell starts to float about.
When the delicious chicken goes into my mouth,
There it rests, till it floats down south.

Nazifa Chowdhury (11)
Mulberry School for Girls

War!

Can you hear the clashes of swords and spears?
Nothing but metal noises running through your ears.

People are killing, people are dying,
Children are hurt and you hear them crying.

Spreading hate and destroying everything,
I ask myself, is life worth living?

Do people live to see this day?
One by one, everyone passing away.

What do people gain from all this?
Can't a person get a little peace?

Ripping people's bodies apart,
Tearing up their hearts.

Shedding a person's blood,
Burying them under the mud.

Being locked up in a cell,
Life is like a living hell.

What will make this a better place?
Seeing smiles on people's face.

War causes *pollution!*
Peace is the only *solution!*

Rajna Begum (11)
Mulberry School for Girls

Chips, Chips, Chips!

They haven't any bones,
They haven't any pips,
They're really mushy inside
That's why I like chips!

They fill me up when I'm hungry,
Or cheer me up when I'm down,
I can't believe how delicious they are
How very pleased I am!

I also love the crusty outside,
They make my mouth go *crunch*
I can even hear them churning in my mouth
They're easy and so fun to munch!

Last of all I'd like to say,
I could have chips every day.
About that I'm not entirely sure,
'Cos I don't think I like chips anymore!

Nayema Begum (11)
Mulberry School for Girls

What Am I?

What am I?
I am not a human
But I have a body
Made of light,
I shine so bright
The stars are my friends
And I am grateful
For I watch over you
And protect you from all evil
What am I?
(An Angel.)

Jahanara Begum (12)
Mulberry School for Girls

Untitled

When you hear this it'll make you feel weak
Spine tingles, mind jingles, wanna drop to your feet.
Listen up, volume down, express on without beat
Don't like it, find elsewhere, UK poem, unique

Write with this blue and red pen
Make any paper, notebook bigger than Ben
From the sheet to your eyes it gets sent
Feel so good you need to look again

Other poems overrated, but look so basic
It's your time, think don't waste it!
Don't rush yourself, slow down and pace it
Calm down, this ain't the Grand Prix

The mind thinks, the body acts
(Can't control it) I'm doing just that
Rearrange twisted facts
Which you can roll up and feed to your cats.

This is more than just free verse
Put it on the old converse
Select the new one on the reverse
Heard it, seen it, another last verse.

Luke Nakhid
Norlington School

Autumn

As I walk through the park, I hear conkers clicking and clacking,
As I stride through the long grass, I hear the sound of crickets
                                                    Singing,
As I wander back home I smell bonfires burning,
The wonderful sunsets of orange, purple and pink
Fill me with imagination,
And my hand goes numb as I touch my frosted window.

Tara Odeinde (11)
Notting Hill & Ealing High School

My Ice Cream

I is for ice cream, a comforting reward
C is for chocolate, so greatly adored
E is for enormous, creamy and enticing.

C is for caramel, with sprinkles for icing
R is for raspberry, my favourite flavour.
E is for every taste you can think of to savour
A is for all the colours of the rainbow smeared on my face
M is for mad, 'cause if you don't like ice cream you are

a nut case!

Francesca Barberis (11)
Notting Hill & Ealing High School

The Man Who Loved To Eat

There was once a man, who loved to eat,
Who never usually used his feet
He just sat there and ate and ate,
Shouting, 'With all this food, I need another plate.'
He slept in the café where he could smell the food,
When he had his breakfast he would be very rude
He would burp and fart,
Without the smallest alert!
He would say, 'It was the bacon and eggs.'
So everyone started bringing pegs!
He was only quiet when eating his lunch,
Washed down with a cocktail punch,
Then came a massive ice cream,
When he saw this, the strange man beamed!
After a spoonful,
He said, 'I'm full.'
But then went as red as a rag to a bull!
And disgustingly began to drool,
And all so sudden he went pop off his feet
And that was the end of the man who loved to eat!

Josephine Swoboda (11)
Notting Hill & Ealing High School

Autumn Stroll

A utumn will always be my favourite month
U nder the trees that sway all day
T hey shed leaves that fall gracefully to the ground.
U nderstanding what is to come, the hedgehog wanders
                                    Off to his shelter.
M others watch as their children play amongst the brown,
                        Yellow and orange Post-it notes
N obody thinks about the harsh winter ahead,
            As the beauty of autumn is too overpowering.

S uddenly, one day the dread winds blow
T he sun no longer warms the arms of the trees
R otten leaves pile up and smell like death
O h how the trees mourn over their children's bodies
L eft alone until spring brings new life
L arks will return and call in the spring.

Leila Brown (11)
Notting Hill & Ealing High School

Autumn

Season of conkers and dancing tree tops,
Swirling colours falling to the ground,
The first horse chestnut to crack its casing
While hungry eyes watch without a sound.

Season of harvests and tumbling apples,
Over-ripe fruit lying sprawled on the lawn,
The last of the wheat is being collected,
Making way for new crops to be born.

Season of darkness and dying embers,
The blazing fire makes a glorious sight,
While the sun bids farewell to the autumn
The last of the day fades into night.

Hannah Greenstreet (11)
Notting Hill & Ealing High School

Spinach And Brussels Sprouts

'What's your favourite food?' they say,
'I really would like to know.'
Fish and chips, hot salsa dips,
Roasted lamb, slices of ham,
Bacon and eggs, chicken legs,
Chocolate flakes, lemon cakes,
What wonderful food galore!
Every day it's always the same,
At break time they say to me,
'What is your favourite food,'
They say,
'What is your favourite food?'
I think and think, but no such luck,
And break time is quickly ending,
So as the bell rings, I announce,
'Spinach and Brussels sprouts!'

Natalie Neil (11)
Notting Hill & Ealing High School

Autumn

Autumn leaves falling all around
Yellow, red, orange and brown,
All falling to the ground.

The trees are looking bare
And all the leaves are brittle
And easy to tear.

It's bleak and windy and cold
But the leaves aren't standing bold
And the trees are looking old.

But everyone's happy and cheerful
For autumn's just begun.

Charlotte Payne (11)
Notting Hill & Ealing High School

Grandma's Cooking!

The scent is drifting up the stairs
Entering all the rooms,
I open every single window, in every single room!
But still the smell is there, and staying there for good.
The high shrill from below calling,
'The food is ready, come and eat
My most wonderful and delicious feast!'
Already feeling that little bit sick,
Taking semi-pigeon steps in small, wiggly lines,
Just to take a longer time.
Not knowing what to say or do,
'I need the toilet,' no that's no good.
Praying for my mum's return
A trip to Pizza Hut would be my prayer returned.
I look at it, just sitting there
No words could describe it
My grandma smiled as if saying:
'Nothing's wrong with it I promise'.
But I was not so sure
I heard a key turn in the door,
Then jumped up with joy, someone had come to save me!
But then I saw the old man's face
It was just my dear grandpa
Only then did I know I was not in luck and he said,
'I'm just in time to join you ladies,
Let's go and eat what's on the table!'

Milina Magnus (11)
Notting Hill & Ealing High School

Oh Christmas Dinner!

Oh Christmas dinner!
Thought John one morning,
As he climbed out of bed,
Stretching and yawning.
He went downstairs,
To where Mum was cooking.
Then into the living room,
To see his stocking.
It was filled with presents
Right up to the brim,
Then he looked at the Christmas tree,
Which needed a trim!
Oh Christmas dinner!
Sighed John as he ate,
Turkey and stuffing,
Forced down by a date.
All the bread and the chestnuts,
Mince pies and Brussels sprouts,
Almost the whole table,
Went into little John's mouth.
And when finally John sat back in his chair,
He thought, *there must be a way,*
For me to have the joy of Christmas dinner,
Every single day . . .'
'Oh Christmas dinner!'
Said John aloud,
As he gave his mum a Christmas foods list,
She said, 'I can't get all these every day,
But I'll try if you really insist!'
Devils on horsebacks and Christmas puddings,
From then on every day he would scoff!
But soon he was bored of these Christmas treats,
And the novelty seemed to wear off.

When next Christmas came, he felt sick seeing that meal,
That last year had been such a winner!
He stormed out in a huff, but nobody noticed,
For they were enjoying their
    Christmas dinner!

Lorig Chakelian (11)
Notting Hill & Ealing High School

Some Fresh Mozzarella Waiting Just For Me!

I open up the fridge door,
And oh! What do I see?
Some fresh mozzarella waiting just for me.

I ponder, 'Should I steal it?'
You know what, yes I will,
For this mozzarella, my stomach it will fill.

Onto the chopping board it goes,
And oh! to my delight,
The squidgyness is too much, I have to take a bite.

I have to feel it one more time before I eat it all,
It is so soft and delicate, why have I not noticed it before?
I see this chunk before me, it is impossible to ignore.

I cut it into slices and pop one in my mouth,
Then another and another, till every bit is gone,
And now I have none, I feel so forlorn.

Francesca Humphreys (11)
Notting Hill & Ealing High School

Mum's Meals

My favourite meals are Mum's meals,
Which meal today?
A Sunday roast
Or a quick pasta?
But no matter what,
My favourite meals are Mum's meals.

Here comes the starter,
Ooh! A Jamie Oliver
To make a beginning,
But no matter what,
My favourite meals are Mum's meals.

Now for the main course,
Comes at you hot and proud,
Mum's own creation, Poacher's Pie,
But no matter what,
My favourite meals are Mum's meals.

Which pudding shall it be?
A sugary meringue
Or a lush apple crumble?
Who made this?
You're about to find out
Because no matter what
My favourite puddings are *my* puddings!

Miranda Bain (11)
Notting Hill & Ealing High School

Autumn Makes Me Want To Smile

Autumn is a necklace of pure gold,
A piece of jewellery that beholds utmost beauty,
Autumn is a breeze of fresh, sweet air,
Blowing through my ebony locks.

Autumn reminds me of a blazing fire,
Dancing in front of a smiling audience,
Autumn reminds me of fireworks,
Each whistling to their own unique tune.

Autumn smells like apple pie,
Warming in the oven,
Autumn smells like warm toast,
Smeared with sticky honey.

Autumn feels like twigs and leaves,
Cracking under one's feet,
Autumn feels like love and laughter,
Mixed in one ball of excitement,
Too big to fit into a trillion poems.

Autumn makes me want to smile.

Livia Wang (11)
Notting Hill & Ealing High School

Fast Food

Burgers, fries and milkshake,
Tasty and welcoming to your mouth.
Always eager to spend and spend
It drives your parents round the bend.
You've never had anything like it before
Soon you realise you want it more and more.

In this disguise you won't see,
That this food is not at all healthy.
Sure it's great, it's hard to hate
But eat it too much and watch yourself grow.
You'll end up looking like Santa Claus, oh no, no.

So many delicious desserts you can buy
Hot and crumbly apple pie
Cold and creamy ice cream
You love it a lot,
Mmm it's gorgeous
Thank you ever so much.

How much food
How much do you eat?
Think about it, it's not that good a treat.
You must now realise how unhealthy it is.
You may think this food is ever so tasty
But wait and think about it, don't be too hasty.

Free goodies, lots of gifts
So much fun to play with
Also that bursting surprise before you open it
That's what you get when you get a kids' meal.
Think about it, it's a two for one deal.

All the free toys, it's just a compromise
You pay so much for all this weight.
Look at yourself in the mirror
You look such a state
Throw all that fatty food in the bin
You'll feel great!

Gurneek Sehmbhi (11)
Notting Hill & Ealing High School

Where Should We Go Out To Eat?

In my family, it's very hard to find a place to eat
Dad can't have milk, I don't eat wheat.
Noah needs a high chair, Carolyn doesn't do sweet
And not forgetting Hannah who doesn't eat meat.

Let's go to Okawari, it's been a while since we've been there
'No,' said Dad, 'they don't own a high chair.
And remember the last time when we were there?
Noah crawled around and pulled some old guy's hair.'
'Okay then, not there.'

'I know, let's go to KFC
They have nice food,' I shouted with glee.
'But remember we're banned because of last year
Hannah released all the chickens and yelled at the cashier.'
'Okay then, not there.'

'How about pizza,' Hannah hopefully said
'No they have wheat in the pizza base bread,
That's an idea, but remember before
When Sophie threw up all over the floor?'
'Okay then, not there.'

'Let's go out for ice cream,' I said cunningly
'No,' Carolyn said extremely annoyingly
'Your father can't eat that sort of stuff,' and then said with a shiver,
'And remember how bad sugar is for your liver.'

We sat there and pondered for a while
Then suddenly with a smile
A thought came to me with incredible ease
'I know, let's all go out for Chinese.'

Sophie Wilk (11)
Notting Hill & Ealing High School

The Blackberry

The seeds are flung into the damp soil,
Like gloomy stars on a tranquil night,
Reaching up like wounded soldiers
They devour water and luminous light.

Time zooms by and the blistering sun beams,
The ferocious heat locks up the rain,
Squirrels scamper into the shade,
The petrified bush survives scorching pain.

The plants that are seeds grow rapidly,
Colourful leaves glide daintily down,
A shiver creeps up the bare trees,
The howling sneers at my burning frown.

Vigorous storms hassle all creatures,
Snow now rules any beautiful green,
The dilapidated bush cries,
Bitter cold stabs exhilarating scenes.

The dismal bush recovers slowly,
Its one feeble stem gains all power,
The smell of mud wafts through the air,
Humming bees buzz proudly round flowers.

Blackberries ripen all over the bush,
Like intricate pearls on a necklace,
They are all picked except for one,
The scent of nectar sleeps on my face.

The desolate berry stands alone,
Gloomy shrouds of mist cloud around her,
As she still remains forgotten . . .
Suddenly a hand swoops out and grabs her.

A tongue gets ready to lick the juice,
Grinding sharp teeth eagerly prepare,
Warm breath attacks the scrumptious fruit,
The irresistible aroma flares.

The sweet and delicious berry waits,
Plop into the mouth, about to drown . . .
Saliva mixes with the taste,
The last bits of berry slip down, down, down.

Saijal Reahal (11)
Notting Hill & Ealing High School

Autumn Poem

Ruby-red leaves and hazel-coloured conkers,
These are the things I see in autumn,
Droplets of rain falling from the sky,
And the trees swaying in the gentle autumn breeze,
These are the things I see in autumn.

Whistling wind and thundery rain,
These are the things I hear in autumn,
Smashing conkers as they fall from the trees,
These are the things I hear in autumn.

Crispy leaves from the trees,
These are the things I touch in autumn,
Hard, round conkers, ready to be smashed,
These are the things I touch in autumn.

Hot school dinners, to keep us warm,
These are the things I taste in autumn.

Hot burning logs from someone's bonfire,
These are the things I smell in autumn.

Sophie Hart (11)
Notting Hill & Ealing High School

Fasting On Yom Kippur

(The Jewish day of atonement)

Cold, numb, bored,
In this place that we pray.
Cold, numb, bored,
My hunger is here to stay.
Five more hours until I can eat.

Bored, numb, cold,
Just watching the singers.
Bored, numb, cold,
How my hunger lingers.
Four more hours until I can eat.

Numb, bored, cold,
Reading the Hebrew prayer book.
Numb, bored, cold,
Then my stomach shook
Three more hours until I can eat.

Bored, cold, numb.
Food is on my mind.
Bored, cold, numb,
If I daydream I can find -
Chocolate and cherries and hot, melting cheese.
Pasta and pizza and chicken with peas.
Two more hours until I can eat.

Cold, bored, numb,
Daydreams bring on hunger pains.
Cold, bored, numb,
The hole in my stomach is in flames,
One more hour until I can eat.

The service is over
Freedom! Elation!
I rush hungrily to see my relation.

The door opens wide
The smell overcomes me.
Fish and potatoes are being fried
And brewing strong herbal tea
My stomach lurches in anticipation.

The soup slips down my throat
It feels like I've wrapped around a warm winter coat.
Heavenly sensations of delicate fish
Fulfils my hungriest wish.
I warmly sink into chocolate cake dreams.

The fasting is finished,
The day is complete
My hunger diminished
I'm content and replete
Food never tasted so good.

Georgia Posner (12)
Notting Hill & Ealing High School

Autumn O Autumn

Autumn, O, autumn
How your colours glow
Whilst your soft winds blow
On the hills, across the fields
And through the rustling trees.

Autumn, O, autumn
Colours of gold, orange and red
Blankets the Earth from toe to head
The musty air lurks round every corner
Weakening the sunshine as the days get shorter.

Autumn, O, autumn
Your bountiful harvest of fruits and grain
Gathered before the winter's rain
Children enjoying your falling leaves
Eating delicious toffee apples when they please.

Millie Chesson (11)
Notting Hill & Ealing High School

Fast Food

Out at the shops, desperate for lunch,
What can I find that I can munch?
I glance around, what can be found?
I'm so hungry it must be quick,
Which of these options should I pick?

Should I have burger and chips?
No such food shall pass my lips!
I hate the pickle, I'm too fickle!
What about nuggets or fish,
Not a tremendously tasty dish.

Pizza with toppings of mushroom and rocket,
Oh no! Not enough change in my pocket,
I could have a Coke, what a joke!
BBQ chicken dipped in sauce,
Much too messy to eat of course!

A sandwich shop is what I need,
A far healthier option, indeed,
A place is near, my choice is clear,
Tuna and mayo with salad and corn,
The first thing I've eaten since breakfast at dawn!

Frances Worthington (11)
Notting Hill & Ealing High School

Happy Poem

A happy colour is red
A happy taste is strawberries
A happy memory is reading a book
A happy sight is my computer
A happy sound is the rain dripping on the windowpanes
A happy smell is my mum's cooking.

Fatima Freifer (11)
Phoenix High School

Football ABC Poetry

A is for Alan Smith, Man Utd striker!
B is for Barcelona, a Spanish club!
C is for Cristiano Ronaldo, my favourite player!
D is for David Beckham, England skipper!
E is for Enhee, a future footballer!
F is for Fulham, who have the youngest manager in the Premiership!
G is for Ryan Giggs, he's in my team!
H is for Henrik Larsson, a Swede!
I is for Ireland, not really bad!
J is for Jonathan Woodgate, a Real Madrid defender!
K is for Roy Keane, the captain of my team!
L is for Freddie Ljungberg, another Swede!
M is for Manchester United, my team!
O is for Ole Gunnar Solskjaer, my injured striker!
P is for Portsmouth, they beat my team!
Q is for Nigel Quashie!
R is for Real Madrid, the biggest club in the whole world!
S is for Paul Scholes, retired from international duty!
T is for Thierry Henry, a French!
U is for Ukraine, Andriy Shevchenko of AC Milan!
V is for Berti Vogts, dropped down!
W is for Wayne Rooney, the most expensive Premier League striker!
X is for Xabi Alonso, a Spanish!
Y is for Luke Young, a Charlton one!
Z is for Zinedine Zidane, best footballer of the year!

Enhbadrah Batkhuyag (11)
Phoenix High School

Success

Why do you think everything of yours goes wrong?
Why do you think success is not yours?
Cheer up! People succeed because they are destined to.
Most people succeed because they are determined to.
Choose your place, which one are you?
Stand up to your goals, make your time utilised.
Make this little saying your motto,
'Opportunity comes but once so utilise the time at your disposal.'
Say to yourself I can make it, use your heart to say your motto.

Arafat Ariori (12)
Phoenix High School

The Wind

The wind is like an invisible cheetah
So fast you can't see it
It whistles through the trees
And tugs on its branches
It rips off the leaves
And throws them like a blanket on the ground
It makes windows rattle
And doors slam shut
It raises waves to new heights
Making boats head to shore
No warning when it comes
No warning when it goes
At first just a light breeze
And then suddenly the full force hits you
Sending shivers down your spine
As if it's seeking revenge . . .

Gursharon Dhariwal (13)
Phoenix High School

Love

Love would taste sherbet sweet but sometimes sour.
It would also taste like red, sloppy jam spreading over the bread.

Love would smell like a baking cake.
Love would sound like a microwave pinging to tell you
your food is ready.

Love would feel like jelly, bouncy yet yummy,
Or clouds, soft, yet comfortable.

Love would look like blossom growing on a tree
Or a delicious creamy split bun with a layer of strawberry jam
down the middle.

Jennifer Miles (11)
Phoenix High School

School Again

Playground school bell rings again
Rain clouds come to play again
If I smile and don't believe
They don't know the secret from within school again.
Endless corridors to walk through
Endless subjects to learn till you forget
I know this stuff is meant to help me
But maybe, just maybe if everyone will stop pressuring me,
Maybe then I'll understand.
School again.
What really upsets me
Is everyone walking around
With a mum or dad
Or even both
And I'm stuck with
No one
School again.

Felicia Dosunmu (12)
Phoenix High School

My Poem

I love the way you touch me
So soft and sensuously
It makes me tingle all over.

I love the way you kiss me
It starts a fire deep down inside me,
And makes me yearn for you even more.

I love the way you look at me
It makes me feel beautiful and treasured
Most of all I love the way you love me.

When you walk in, my whole day gets better
And even when you're not with me
You're in my thoughts always.

It doesn't matter what we do have or what we don't have
The most important thing is we have each other
And no one can take that away.

I am the luckiest person in the world
And I don't need or want anything
But you beside me, loving me, to the end of our days.

Dexter Ganpot (14)
Phoenix High School

The Dark Night

The dark night starts to fall,
And my mummy starts to call.
I turn around with shivers up my spine
When I realise the time.
I start to run as it gets darker
I run and bump into Mr Parker.
I run indoors and into bed.
'Goodnight dear,' my mummy said.

Kaliegh Gilbert (12)
Phoenix High School

Little White Kitten

Little white kitten with round marble eyes
All springing and leaping and jumping surprise.
Soft as cotton, light as a feather,
Outside playing whatever the weather.

She's so cute, more than you ever could say
Laying by the fire every single day.
This kitten is so full of puff
Round and white and covered in fluff.

This little kitten she jumps all around
Up to the ceiling and down to the ground,
In the morning she's so down and low
Because she knows I have to go.

Charlotte Becker (13)
Phoenix High School

Little Sisters

L ittle sisters are so annoying
I wonder what their purpose in life cold be
T hough maybe it's to destroy my life
T hink that's what it could be
L ittle sisters are evil
E vil is their middle name.

S ometimes I wonder what they think of me
I could be their favourite game
S heer enjoyment is what they get from me
T rying to keep away from them
E nough to tire anyone
R estless they become after a while
S isters, can be so annoying.

Ayan Yusuf (12)
Phoenix High School

Peace, Love And Respect

I want to be somewhere
I want to live somewhere
Somewhere in peace
But where is the peace?
Here or there
Or shall I say I can't find that place?

I want to see somewhere
I want to be somewhere
Somewhere where people do one thing
That thing is love and respect.

Give me love and support when I need their help
Give me respect when I helped them.

Where can I find this place?
Where is this place?

Arian Nemani (14)
Phoenix High School

The Willow Tree

Near the lake,
It stands with long thin branches,
Its narrow leaves stretched out wide,
The willow tree is always there,
No matter where or when,
Its beauty is always shining,
Which changes your mood and mind,
And if you ever feel lonely,
The willow tree is always there for you,
The lake is smooth and calm,
The leaves are always green,
The branches are always thin,
And the sight makes you grin.

Aimal Mazidi (12)
Phoenix High School

Spring

The sun rises to start a new day
It brings a shine to the trees and birds
They are singing gracefully
And the seagulls flying away
Natural
I feel it.

I hear my alarm clock going off,
I feel my hands rubbing into my eyes
I hit my alarm cock with a bang
And stand up pushing my blanket away
My life
I know it!

Looking outside my window makes me feel natural
Seeing the sun shining on the birds making them glisten
Feeling the breeze going across my face
And hearing the wonderful noise the birds make
Natural
I feel it.

I go downstairs feeling happy and seeing what today could be like,
Sitting on my chair, picking up my toast and biting it,
Hearing a loud *crunch!*
Forgetting to put on my slippers, I feel the coldness going up my feet
Going outside and seeing the buds of a flower open in slow motion.

> *Spring has come.*

Kluloud Jama (11)
Phoenix High School

Oh Gentle One

Oh gentle one, why did you leave me here
Heartbroken and panic-stricken.

Oh gentle one, I am becoming a person
A person I always despised.

I wanted to do your memory proud
But I am becoming self-centred and selfish
A person I would have condemned.

Oh gentle one, I let those evil spirits in
Let them rack my soul with thoughts of self-worth
I let them change me; I'm not who I used to be.

Oh gentle one, I hurt the ones I love
And I care what worthless people think of me
Where did my confidence go?

Oh gentle one, I let those feelings drain me
Feelings of self-pity and depression
They killed my heart and soul.

I was a free spirit, I am now a prisoner in my own mind.

Oh gentle one, come back and release me from this prison
The prison that is me.

Sivanna Sherry (14)
Phoenix High School

Because Of War!

The noise, the screaming, the bullets zooming past;
Then you turn around, *boom!* There's a blast.
You fall back onto the floor;
You shout out, *'No more! No more!'*

Nobody listens or nobody hears;
You look around as smoke clears.
You see the guns blazing and the people shouting;
You start to crawl as your fears are mounting.

Then you hear the bullet, you feel the pain;
You cry out in disbelief, as it starts to rain.
Your back is bleeding, you feel all cold;
You close your eyes, you're feeling old.

You open your eyes, try to stand;
You hear a bullet, hits your hand.
You give up hope, fall to the ground;
Your head starts to spin round and round.

You know what's happening, you know you're going;
Your vision's blurred, your hearing's slowing.
You take your last breath, as you're feeling numb;
You just whisper, 'I'm coming Mum.'

Aydrous Yousuf (14)
Phoenix High School

The World Is My Shelter

The world is my shelter but is always blocking me out
For the world is all we have today
But the evil just won't fade away
People die and we shed tears
Hate and anger is life's most feared
But when we try to look in time
We think it's only worth a dime
Angels come and take my friends
But this life I live is not yet at an end.

It was not meant to, but it happened
We cried for days but couldn't understand
Why someone out there would take you off this land
The world is evil but we share it
People think they're better and try to declare it
We live in pain and time goes on
But with this creation somewhere something went wrong
We'll stay true as long as we're strong
Even though you're not, I still feel you here
And
Everything happens for a reason, that is now clear
But
I'll pray for the day when love will stay
To watch the children grow and play.

Christina Rankin (14)
Phoenix High School

Wasn't There

I was playing in the park with my mum
Only my mum wasn't there
I was building a castle with my dad
Only my dad wasn't there
My sister and I were going shopping
Only my sister wasn't there
I was going to watch TV with my grandad
Only my grandad wasn't there
I was going to play on the computer with my brother
Only my brother wasn't there
I was going to the cinema with my cousin
Only my cousin wasn't there
They can never be there anymore
Because they are somewhere, where I'm not.

Why can't they be there, I don't understand
I try to play with them
But they don't play back
When I talk to them
They don't talk back
Why has this happened? Why to me?
Why did someone do this?
I don't understand why
Why, oh why
I can't play anymore because it's no fun without them
I can't go out to have fun because it's no fun without them
I can't build castles anymore because it's no fun without them
I can't go to the cinema anymore because it's no fun without them
I want them back, please make them come back
If they don't come back, then I want to go where they are.
I want to be dead.

Reah Cyrus (14)
Phoenix High School

Last Date

I turned up to the station
All excited and new,

I waited, it seemed like an age
Not a sign of you,

My friends said you would let me down
'You don't know him!'
I shouted.

They even had a show of hands
I guess I was out-voted.

Now it's time to walk away,
It seems you're not just late

What should I say?
'Had a great day.'
On our imaginary last date.

Tanika Yearwood (11)
Phoenix High School

Mama Land

Close my eyes, it's a vision, my imagination
Green pastures, fresh water streams
Flow through the grass lands.

Open my eyes, I see blood
Blood shed.
Kids orphaned, lands deserted
Look around, graves.

She bares nothing but lost souls.
She suckled her breasts to a
Swept away generation,
My generation . . .

Gloria Giramiya (14)
Phoenix High School

The Rage

It builds up inside you,
But you'll never let it out.
The hate and anger you feel grows,
But you don't scream or shout.

The pain and suffering well up inside you,
But you cannot cry.
You just bottle it up,
And wonder why.

You're filled with sadness,
Thinking about times past.
If you don't release these feelings
You know that the rage will last.

You're full of bitterness,
Which slowly consumes you.
You're filled with doubt,
But you must let it out.

You need to let them know,
Before you can truly let go.

Sarah Militello (15)
Phoenix High School

Ghosts

Creaking floorboards,
Through the night,
Nothing here,
Or a soul in sight,
Whisper, whisper,
That's all I can hear,
I wonder if a ghost is near?

Rachel Graver (13)
Phoenix High School

True Love

How is love meant to be
It isn't just brothers, sisters and our family,
It's people in our community
Now I'm going to tell you what love is to me.

It isn't when you told me so
It wasn't when I asked you out and you said, 'No.'
It ain't when I tied your bow
And it definitely isn't when *you* rocked the boat.

True love is meant to be strong
And look it's going awfully wrong.
Where did you get this rubbish from?
I thought about making this poem into a rap song.

You said you loved me too many times,
As I say you do the crime, you do the time
But to you this isn't a crime
To you this is a silly old rhyme.

You always used to give me a shove
And of course I thought that it was love
But no, it is this poem that is *true love*.

Chloe Parke-Rawlins (11)
Phoenix High School

Summer

S un comes out and shines on us
U sually it is sunny but in England sometimes it is raining
M y favourite season is summer
M ango is my favourite fruit
E verywhere is full of smiles
R ainbows come out when it is raining and sunny.

Marzia Ahmadi (11)
Phoenix High School

Limericks

There once was a guy called Bill
Who could never keep still
One day he got a gun
He was loaded with rum
And shot a guy called Dill!

There once was a guy called Larry
Who thought his name was Harry
Who went and got a drink
And that got him to think
What if his name was Barry!

Samuel Cotter (14)
Phoenix High School

My Last Thoughts

I sit and wait
Through my hand runs the blade
My mind was gone
I saw my bone
I saw a face
I felt encased
It was strange
I ranged
My tears were dry
I don't know why
But I thought about my life
I remember a knife
With one I ruined my life
Then I was blind
But now it's too late
To change something.

Agne Sausdravaite (14)
Phoenix High School

The Midnight Beast

12 o'clock sharp
I've turned into a beast
Creeping down the stairs
For my midnight feast.

Looking in the cupboard
There's lots of tinned foods
I think I'll try the freezer
For a food that suits my mood.

Opening the freezer
I get a shiver down my spine
Taking out the nuggets
Taking out nine.

I shove them in the oven
How long will it take?
I'm getting quite sleepy
Will I stay awake?

I'm getting quite hungry
And the nuggets aren't ready
I grab a packet of crisps
But I'll take it steady.

I did not do what I said
But scoffed them down my throat
I am so fat and like a pig
That in water I can't float.

I'm sure they're ready now
But the bell hasn't rung
I'll get them out I think
Before I burn my tongue.

I've finished my nuggets
That was a nice midnight meal
I might come down tomorrow night
But I'll see how I feel.

I'm back upstairs
All tucked up in bed
My belly's stopped rumbling
Now it's been fed.

Pavneet Dhariwal (12)
Phoenix High School

Neva 4get U!

It's been a day and even still
Your memory lingers on
Your memory so very strongly felt
It's hard to believe that you've gone.

Not gone in spirit, but in a physical sense
Because somehow you're still alive
In our hearts,
In our minds,
In the tears we've all cried.

Some didn't know you personally,
Yet still feel the sting of that day
That day the heavens
Opened their gates
And took an angel away.

Very angelic you were,
Style and grace all of your own
The reason your life ended so suddenly
Was because of a mobile phone.

You had so much to live for,
So much more to do
Now you'll just grace the heavens
While Jesus watches over you.

R I P.

Tahire Simnica (15)
Phoenix High School

Beach Raiders

The sun dawns, day starting anew,
Waves advance, retreat, day after day,
Shifting sands, damp from morning dew,
The light comes, chasing shadows away.

A timeless moment, frozen on the spot,
A perfect moment, one that will last,
A silent moment, break it will not,
An eternal moment, only from the past.

The sun rises high, beacon of the lands,
Seen by all below, busy in their scrawl,
Through no bounds, over the sands,
Ignorance reigns, ruling them all.

A ruined moment, nothing goes, no spoil,
A normal moment, happens every day,
A noisy moment, crying out in toil,
A long moment, for that is how they stay.

The day ends, the sun sets,
Light retreats, giving way to dark,
In darkness shows, drops no regrets,
Peace returns, but raiders left mark.

A new moment, one so serene,
A fresh moment, lightning the heart,
A last moment, day now unseen,
A first moment, fresh for a new start.

Joseph Cotter (15)
Phoenix High School

Poem

I achieved my handwriting
I tried and tried, sure
I messed up a few times but
I got it in the end.

I showed my mum and my friends
And they said, 'That's very nice handwriting.'
I felt good.

So people out there don't stop trying
'Cos you will get there in the end,
So don't stop trying, you will never fail!

Ashleigh Britnell (12)
Phoenix High School

People Today

People today are just typical.
I guess that's how it goes, treat people like you want to be treated
Or that's what my mum told me but I never listened to her,
So I ended on the street after I left school and my mum's house.
I behaved towards people badly and I got this in return.
Now I'm living from the scraps of my fingernails,
Begging and stealing most of the time.
Rarely do I get a penny from a passer-by.
Then I just stand and ask myself why.
Just like my friend who just passed away,
I like the busy streets and the hustle and bustle.
But to me being rich is just mythical.
People today, they are just typical.

Mohammed Ahmed (11)
Rokeby School

Homeless Person

What do I do? Live
It's my culture
No one understands me
It's like I'm a shadow
I don't understand
I just want friends
Just like an ordinary person
What did I do wrong?
There's a boy up the street
Who hates me in fear.
I'm not bad
Not like that div.
What do I do? Live.

Elliott Mower (11)
Rokeby School

Multicoloured World

People from around the world
We are all the same
We start off young
And end up old,
And we live altogether
In a multicultural world.

People from the north,
People from the south,
People from the east
People from the west.

Everyone together
All as one
Helping each other
Our job is done.

Iasai Patel (13)
Rokeby School

Homeless

I am homeless on the streets.
No more warmth or family treats.
Begging and borrowing off passers-by.
'I wish I wasn't homeless,' I cry.
Dirty clothes, pale is my skin.
I look like rubbish that came out the bin.
Tired and lonely, got no friends.
Got to find shelter for my daily trends.
Trying hard to find a room,
Knocking at a door, nothing till June.
Desperate and lonely, feeling so down.
Everywhere I look I feel like a clown.
So all you homeless people out here
Don't look down, don't cry a tear.
I am homeless on the streets.

Desmond Mitchell
Rokeby School

A Homeless Life

Oh my gosh, what a life!
Sitting there near the bin
What else to do? Well I just go to a store
And steal food.
I hate this life, feel like dying.
I used to be a cleaner, but they didn't give
Me much so I began to steal.
Got nine years.
After jail went crazy with drugs.
Lost my ID, licence and house.
Friends ignore me.
I feel like killing someone with a knife.
Oh my gosh, what a life!

Zanis Zilvinskis (12)
Rokeby School

Should I Live, Should I Die

Should I live, should I die?
I have not much to eat,
I have not much to say,
Because I'm a teenager, I'm quite vulnerable,
In a month I usually earn £1 or £3,
I ran away from home because I was treated very strict,
Even worse it's coming up to winter, will I live or die?
I beg for money but some people swear at me,
I stole three times and got caught only once,
I take drugs and drink alcohol,
I steal, I take drugs and lie,
Should I live, should I die?

Abdul Rahman Umar
Rokeby School

Poem Of The Homeless

What did I do?
I tried my absolute best
So why didn't they love me?
I thought I made them pleased
Or maybe I didn't help them in any way.
Now I'm all alone,
Eating scraps out of dustbins
Sleeping under cardboard boxes,
I'm only ten. And human;
Why does this have to happen to me? I'm scared.
There's just something I need to know,
Something I've needed to know for ages.
What did I do?

Segun Owode-Oyelaja
Rokeby School

The Stars At Night

I look up into the star-filled sky
I see not a single soul passing by.
Every night I decide that I just might
Carry on and continue my homeless fight.
I don't want to sleep on the outside floor
But my family: they've shown me the door.
Now all I want is just a friend,
Who supports me right to my end.
For food and water I have to beg or steal
And I end up with the worst of meals.
I won't give up and I will stay strong,
I don't know if I'll live for very long.
        As I look up into the empty sky at night.

Muntakim Abdal (11)
Rokeby School

His First Day At School

He walked into the classroom,
And saw a flood of white,
He scanned through the room
There were no black boys in sight.

He sat down,
On a table all alone,
He put his head in his arms,
Wishing he had never left home.

He listened to what the teacher said,
But couldn't understand a word,
He wished he could fly away,
Flap his wings like a bird.

Imran Khan (12)
Rokeby School

Black What's That?

Black, what's that?
All white people used to say
They treated us like crap
Every single day.

Now all around the world there is peace,
Everyone gets along
No fighting like in the Middle East,
Listen to this wise song.

But there used to be a world full of hatred,
Where coloured and white didn't get along.
Whites were treated like they were sacred,
And the coloured were part of the throng.

Luckily the world has changed
And I thank God every day.
Living in England is great,
I hope things stay this way.

So when you're enjoying your games,
Thank God for providing.
Pray that things stay the same
And no matter what colour, we'll be smiling.

Isaac Antwi-Boateng
Rokeby School

Heartache

If only I didn't have to live this day,
The agony, the pain, the anguish,
Why did she have to do this to me?

She kept twisting and turning,
Slithering and sliding,
I tried to get on top
But it just didn't happen
I screamed at her hoping it would help.

I tried to look away
But the excitement kept me looking,
Kept me hanging on
To the very edge of my seat.

I bit off all my fingernails
She was so close,
Yet so far away.

Eventually it had to happen
A thunderbolt crashed through my heart
India had lost the World Cup Final in cricket.

Pritom Roy (13)
Rokeby School

Untitled

I ask myself the same question every day
Why am I a tramp?
I don't even pay my rent
I can't even afford a tent
Because I don't pay my rent
Now I am on the streets
I eat the skin of people's leftover meat
I feel very ashamed
Now my name is Shame
I hate my game
I ask myself the same question every day
Why am I a tramp?

Benjamin Collier (11)
Rokeby School

A Pea Pod For My Love

This year you will not receive a card or a teddy bear
Or even wine.

This year, I will give you a pea pod
Because it is a place where we can be together
And we will never be apart.
It is like our love, because I love you
And I never want this love to end, ever.

My gift to you is a pea pod
Because it is a picture of us and it is something special to me.
It also smells a bit off, but it will never put you off of me.

Take my gift and keep it close to your heart.
My gift will always be special
So we can always be together.
Remember that it is from me and not anyone else.
Keep it close to you because I will be with you
And you will be with me and we will be together forever.

Ellis Graham (12)
Sarah Bonnell School

The Reason

This year you will not receive a card,
Or a heart,
Or even a flower!

This year, I will give you a seed,
Because it is always growing,
And forms something special!
It is like our love,
Because it is always flowing
Like a stream singing!

A seed grows like our love
And that is the reason,
My gift to you is a seed,
Because it says that my heart bleeds,
Like our love it causes pain,
And like when it is attacked
By a weed!

It also shows how we can get through
It all and blossom,
And that is a fact!

Pain and heartache,
Can turn to blossoms,
So that is the reason!

Take my gift and keep it close to your heart,
My gift will always be alive
Like our love!
Remember that it can also die,
So protect my gift
Protect our love!

Love lives,
Love dies,
This is the reason . . .
     For my gift!

Eliis Vincent (13)
Sarah Bonnell School

My Gift To You

This year you will not receive
A rose,
Or a ring,
Or even a teddy.

This year, I will give you an egg
Because it is hard on the outside
And soft in the inside.

It is like our love,
Because it can compare
Our love with itself.

My gift to you is unusual,
But it can explain
Everything.

It can be cracking and even bleed
Like our love.
It also can be very dangerous.

Keep my gift and keep it close
To your heart.
My gift will always be yours.
Take it, keep it, never hate it.
Remember this like I remember
You!

Sophia Mahmood (13)
Sarah Bonnell School

The Fire Of Love

This year you will not receive a rose
Or chocolates
Or even a card.

This year, I will give you *fire*
Because it is hot and strong like our hearts
And mysterious like our wonderful love
Because it is frightening but calming
Which leads us to a powerful relation
So this year I will give you fire.

My gift to you is fire
Because it is also dangerous, sudden and burning
Like our love
Which burns our souls and feelings
It also is comforting, when cold but can be an
Extreme of heat
With bumpy rocks on the way.

Take my gift and keep it close to your heart
My gift will always be unique and great
Because it will show you the meaning of
Our love
Remember that this fire will keep our relation
On the right path.

Shima Suleman
Sarah Bonnell School

Our Love

This year you will not receive,
Chocolates, roses and candles.

This year I will give you the stars
Because they burn forever like our love,
They are like our love because,
They are bright and mysterious,
And they light up the sky like you
Light up my heart.

My gift to you is the stars,
Because they burn how it burns me,
When we are apart,
They also blind me as our love is blind.

Take my gift and keep it close to your heart
My gift will always be burning on like our love,
Through eternity.
Remember that I will always love you,
And you will always be in my heart.

Emma Partridge (13)
Sarah Bonnell School

A Venus Flytrap

This year you will not receive roses
or wine
or even chocolate.

This year, I will give you a Venus flytrap
because it is: in exotic places like love,
it will capture you just like love
and has lots of colours just like love.

It is like our love because it symbolises:
foreverness, togetherness and love.

My gift to you is a Venus flytrap
because it symbolises: love when it is trapped,
dangerous when you get pricked
and angry like our love when arguments occur.

Take my gift and keep it close to your heart.
My gift will always be with you and a reminder of our love.
Remember that we were trapped and captured in love.

Rabia Mahmood (13)
Sarah Bonnell School

A Gift For You

This year you will not receive chocolates
Or a card
Or even a beautiful red rose.

This year, I will give you a cat
Because it is,
A cute furry animal which no one can ever have.
It is like our love,
Because cats are sweet,
And our love can also be sweet.

My gift to you is dangerous
Because it can
Be fierce and harming just like our love.
It also scratches like love is fighting.

Take my gift and keep it close to your heart.
My gift will always be the symbol of our love.
Remember that this is a sign of love.

Aliya Rafiq (13)
Sarah Bonnell School

A Gift

This year you will not receive roses or
Chocolates or even a card
This year I will give you a star
Because it is bright and colourful.
It is like our love because we're bright
And when we're together we shine.
My gift to you is a star because it has sharp ends
Like us and it isn't always there.
Take my gift and keep it close to your heart.
My gift will always be there sparkling in the sky,
And when you see it,
Always remember me!

Zainab Tailor
Sarah Bonnell School

Volcano Love!

This year you will not receive flowers or clothes or even underwear.
This year I will give you a volcano because it is hot and dormant
And always erupts.
It is like our love because our love has many ups, but many downs.
When it's dormant, it means love is staying and is always around,
When it erupts, remember it means love is gone
And when we're hot it means love can burn, scald, like lava.
My gift to you is sweet,
Because it means love can sometimes hurt and be a treat.
It also means love is meant forever like a volcano.
Take my gift and keep it close to your heart.
My gift will always be there, I know it'll always be close to you.
Remember this and remember me, take this and respect it.

Josephine Asamoah (12)
Sarah Bonnell School

Just Like Our Love

This year you will not receive chocolates
Or a rose
Or even a card.

This year I will give you metal
Because it is hard and unbreakable
It is just like our love
Because it is solid.

My gift to you is metal
Because it is a conductor of love
It is also shiny, just like our love.

Remember that it can get rusty
Just like love.

Sara Velezmoro (12)
Sarah Bonnell School

Like Our Love . . .

Perfume, cards, roses or candles
Naaah

This year I will give you the sea,
Because it is,
Dangerous like our love, sweet like our love,
Peaceful like our love and also can be
Painful like our love.
It is like our love, because our love is dangerous like
Sharks, and sweet like sugar. Our love is also
Peaceful like a calm sea.

My gift to you is the sea,
Because it is wide,
And deep like our long-lasting love and,
No one can ever take away my valuable love.

Take my gift and keep it close to your heart,
My gift will always be for you,
Remember that our love can never detach or,
No one can ever take away your gift.
Use it, but don't abuse it.

Humera Patel
Sarah Bonnell School

Not An Ordinary Present

This year you will not receive roses,
Or chocolates
Or even a card.

This year, I will give you a lit candle,
Because it is fragrant, dangerous,
An eternal flame.
It is like our love:
It lasts forever, fragrant and colourful.

My gift to you is a lit candle
Because it is hot, dangerous and can
Burn and leave scars.

Take my gift and keep it close to your heart,
My gift will always be fragrant and colourful.
Remember that it describes our love: hot,
Sometimes uncontrollable, but always eternal.

Fatima Riaz
Sarah Bonnell School

Sticky And Sweet!

Chocolates, no
Roses, I don't think so.

This year I'm giving you honey.

Honey is sticky, honey is sweet.
It has the golden aroma of love
Its smooth skin has the soft touch of a new lover.

It is sweet and runny
It promises freshness like the spring of water
It is attractive like the sunflower in the sun-setting garden.
It invites like a freshly brewed champagne

It refreshes your tongue like a freshly tapped palm wine
It gladdens your tummy like love at first sight
It brightens your face like a bright new day.

Its taste is everlasting like true love
But our love is sweeter than honey.

Ayobami Adepoju (12)
Sarah Bonnell School

All Loved Up

This year you will not receive a watch,
Chocolates or even a rose.

This year I will give you a flame,
It represents our love
Because it is hot,
It is bright and it is out of control.

My love burns like a flame with passion for you.
It is never-ending like the love we share.

A flame can have bad points about it
As well as good ones.
Some of them tire, they can be dangerous,
Can burn and scald and it can be hard to handle.

Take my gift and remember it always when you are feeling blue,
It will always be with you.
You might not be able to hold it,
But you can remember it,
That's all that counts!

Touriya Zouita
Sarah Bonnell School

Your Special Present

This year you will not receive jewellery or chocolates,
Or even a Valentine's card.

This year, I will give you the sun
Because it is
Bright, hot and mysterious
It is like our love,
Because you keep me warm, our love is exciting
And sometimes you leave me wondering . . .

My gift to you is the sun,
It burns me when we argue and it is dangerous
It is also blinding like our love.

Take my gift and keep it close to your heart,
My gift will always shine brightly,
And keep you warm.
Remember that I love you and you are very dear to me.

Yasmin Merrin (12)
Sarah Bonnell School

Valentine's Day

Not a red rose, or even a ring,

This year I will give you a sun,
It is red, hot and burning,
Because it can run out of light,
When it's too bright,
Like our love.

My gift to you is the sun,
Because it's beautiful like our love.
Red like our love,
And gets down like our love.

Take my gift and keep it close to your heart,
My gift will always be special to you.
Remember that when you look at it
It'll blind your feelings.

Rukiya Esat
Sarah Bonnell School

Untitled

You're my best sister when you give me money
You're my best sister when you share your honey
You're my best sister when I kick you out of bed
You know you're the best.

You're my best sister to be my only sister
You're my best sister to have no brother
You're my best sister to know you're there
You know you're the best.

You're my best sister you know that's the truth
You're my best sister when there is no route
You're my best sister for ever and always
'Cause you're my only sister.
      Love you always.

Samaarah Butt (14)
Skinners' Company's School for Girls (Lower)

Friends Are

A friend is someone who cares for you
Friends are polite
Friends are kind
Friends are always there for you.

A friend is someone who loves you
Friends are soft
Friends are loveable
Friends are always there for you.

A friend is someone who you trust
Friends are helpful
Friends are grateful
Friends are always there for you.

Öznur Macit (14)
Skinners' Company's School for Girls (Lower)

Great Minds Or Great Fiends?

Albert Einstein liked his wine
Tony Blair is losing his hair
Mother Theresa was really a geezer
Flo' Nightingale wore a cheap veil
Chris Colombus had a nose like a rhombus
Vincent Van Gogh was a bit go-go
Now it seems to me
These lot are off key
I'm done with this
And I need to take a . . .

Dami Taiwo (13)
Skinners' Company's School for Girls (Lower)

My Loyal Mind

Once upon a time I believed that my mind
Was a gift from God.
It disappeared like moonlight
And then came back in the blink of an eye.
My mind was like a cupboard
Storing lots of bits and bobs.
My mind was a cuddly Mummy to me
With a big mind.
My mind was full of loyal deeds
Which charmed like a diamond in the sky.
I could think with it a lot.
It helped me with my exams and tests,
Which popped out all at once,
That's what confused me.
My mind was lying on its wondrous bed,
It was thinking of grace and harmony
Where its soul had gone.
That was the end of my mind!

Akpaljit Kaur (12)
Skinners' Company's School for Girls (Lower)

Success

S *ee* your goal
U *nderstand* the obstacles
C *lear* your mind of doubt
C *reate* a positive mental picture
E *mbrace* the challenge
S *tay* on track
S *how* the world you can do it!

Khadijah Suleman (14)
Skinners' Company's School for Girls (Lower)

Great Minds

Great minds are a hard find
We need to find that special mind!
Some abuse their fame,
Just to be a household name!
All I want to know is who is really true,
As it must be so few.
Are they just copycats?
Wanting a too-big hat.
Too big for their boots is what I mean
Or maybe just too keen?
Some famous people, need to know,
What is wrong and what is right,
But they still are the great minds.

Siobhán O'Brien (13)
Skinners' Company's School for Girls (Lower)

Great Minds

When you look,
There they are.
Are they different,
No they aren't.
It's just the knowledge,
That counts inside.
They're just different,
With extraordinary minds.
They're not different,
They're just wise.
If you cracked your head as hard,
It might be worth a try.
It would not be good enough now.

Krisztina Omoregie (13)
Skinners' Company's School for Girls (Lower)

What Is A Great Mind?

It could be my mother who's taught me a lot.
Like respecting others for who they are
And not for what they've got.

It could be my father, who's taught me to stand up for myself,
To walk with my head held high and to be confident.

It could be my sister, who's taught me never to follow.
To always be myself and at the same time not to be shallow.

It could be my brother, who's taught me not to be shy.
To speak up when necessary and never to lie.

But to me it's all of them above.
As I've learnt from my family all I know, but most of all, love!

Ariana Correia (11)
Skinners' Company's School for Girls (Lower)

Love

Love is like a tube map, inside, outside
Love surrounds, this mystical ground
Highly accusing, mildly insane
Love is luscious, lively and lame.
Love is what makes the world go round
Love is what makes you smile and frown
Up and down, in and out.
Love is an ambition, passed down by many traditions.
Love is a plague, infectious and catching.
Love is a dream, which turns to reality.
Love is hope, there for you when you're feeling blue.
Love is sorrow, a deep cut in your heart
Love equals tears, a stream, a river that leads to an ocean.
Love is life, love is a constant high.
Love is time, love is a game,
Play your cards right and you may win.

Barjinder Kaur (12)
Skinners' Company's School for Girls (Lower)

My Favourite Author

Christopher Pike
I admire his talent
From horror to fantasy
Or a haunted bike.

His expressions
His words,
His morals and lessons.

He's written about vampires
He's written about cats
He's written about witches,
And also scary bats.

Even though it's the end
There's much more to tell
But time has run out.

Amina Patel (11)
Skinners' Company's School for Girls (Lower)

Love Broken Heart Again

You broke my heart
I loved you so
You made me cry
With tender hearts
You crushed my dreams,
And put hers in
My mind is spinning out of control
I loved you so
I loved you so
But now I'm not so sure.

Vanessa Modaku (11)
Skinners' Company's School for Girls (Lower)

The Great Minds

The great minds is a sign
But of what?
Is it love?
Is it care?
Is it the straight path?
I need all three
But I can only have one
Which one will the great minds give me?

The great minds is a sign
But of what?
Is it direction?
If it is, which way?
Left, right?
North, south?
I'm so confused.

The great minds
I need all the signs you're giving
But I'm sure in the end
I will get what I deserve.

The great minds
Will be the best minds
For me.

Anisa Halimah Ahmad (13)
Skinners' Company's School for Girls (Lower)

God's Great Mind

He created the Heavens and the Earth
'Let there be light,' He said and there was light.
What a mighty God, He even made you and me.
He is the King of Kings and Lord of Lords
No one is quite like Him.
He's the Almighty God, that's why I love Him.

Noimot Ishola (12)
Skinners' Company's School for Girls (Lower)

Hooking Mrs Right

Women are, women are, women are,
Women are sensitive,
Women are loving,
Women are understanding to others,
Women love chocolate,
Women love blokes,
Women love watching TV soaps,
Women wear make-up,
Women dress up,
Women wear expensive jewellery to show off,
Women love cats,
Women hate rats,
Women only like cute, furry pets,
Women go clubbing,
Women can dance,
Women fight others over men,
Women can relax,
And calm their souls,
'Cause women know how to let things go.

Naomi Williams (13)
Skinners' Company's School for Girls (Lower)

Naughty Nature

Mother Nature has a great mind
She filled the world with grass and sunshine.
She created sunsets, flowers and rain
Then humans made industrial sites
Oh, what a shame.
At first the world was as fresh as a daisy
But now it's ugly, dirty and crazy.
First it was only Adam and Eve,
Now it's Jane, Mark, Carol and Steve.
Mother Nature has a great mind,
Her only mistake was careless mankind.

Rosie Demellweek (13)
Skinners' Company's School for Girls (Lower)

Great Minds

I believe we all have great minds,
Minds to do what we please,
Some minds we need to lock up and throw away the key.
My mind tells me things, what to do, or what to say,
But without my heart's say I would have to think all day.
You see my heart makes the decisions, decisions that are hard for me.
Whether to go with my mum or follow my friends and be dumb,
I know you know what I'm talking about,
The dilemmas we've all had before,
But if you just follow your mind and your heart,
It will give you the keys to the door,
For we all have great minds,
We just need the time to use them.

Aysha Nicholson (13)
Skinners' Company's School for Girls (Lower)

Many Things I Love About You

I love the way you dance
I love the way you sing
I love the way you laugh
I love the way you drive
I love you x 2
I love the way you play
I love the way you cook
I just love you the way you are
I love the way you dress with
Your blue and red shoes
I love the way you do your hair
I love the way you write
With your strong finger
I love the way you play on your
PlayStations.

Irene Williams (11)
Skinners' Company's School for Girls (Lower)

Weathers

January: New beginning,
             Resolutions
             Snowflakes spinning.

February: Frosty fogs
             Winter shivers
             Fine, warm logs.

March: Blows windy, smells of spring
             Leaves, peek out,
             Brave blackbirds sing.

April: Showers fall soft and slow,
             Earth wakes up,
             And green things grow.

May: Day ribbon round a pole,
             May time babies,
             Lamb and foal.

June: Bring summer blazing in,
             Scent of roses,
             Sun on skin.

July: Joy means schools are out
             Time for picnics
             Heat and drought.

August: Is a time for families to have fun
             Everyone gathers,
             All around the sun.

September: Is boring,
             School opens
             And now it's morning.

October: Is cloudless sky,
             People enjoy
             They have a little nap and lie.

November: Is for friends
            People yell
            It's nearly the end.

December: Is for saying bye,
            Christmas holidays and New Year comes.
            Everyone sighs.

Azmin Hussain (11)
Skinners' Company's School for Girls (Lower)

Great Minds

Great minds are mine and yours.
Yours is mine
And mine's yours.
We think the same
We act the same
And never bring shame.

We've fallen in love
And fitted the glove.
I've kept the memories
That have turned into reality
We never hate
We never rate.

We argue sometimes
But that's the way we show our love
No matter how far away we are
This love will never end.
I love you sis,
For ever and ever.

Hannah Thayer (13)
Skinners' Company's School for Girls (Lower)

Valentine

V alentine, my sweet love, my heart you will always hold.
A ll the treasure in my soul, never again to feel the cold.
L oving you so very much, with years to feel my soul.
E ternity could never be enough, to express my love so bold.
N ever to stray form you, my sweet man is my only god.
T hank you sweetheart, for your love has healed hurt untold.
I n my life you will forever be, with your loving hand to hold.
N o one else could show me so much love, and never let it grow old.
E ternally grateful to my God, for giving me you, with your heart
of gold.

Öznur Macit (14)
Skinners' Company's School for Girls (Lower)

Love And Hate

What does 'love' mean?
What does 'hate' mean?
Are they only words?
I've heard there is a thin line
Between love and hate.
Is this really true?
How can you hate someone you've never loved?
How can you love someone you used to hate?
Your worst enemy could be the person closest to you
So you could be telling your worst enemy your deepest,
darkest secrets.
The person you *think* is your worst enemy could be your
Ideal best friend.
So you can never hate someone you used to love,
Or love someone you used to hate.
What is love?
What is hate?
You decide.

Abena Atta-Dankwa (14)
Skinners' Company's School for Girls (Lower)

Hooking Mrs Right

Women are, women are, women are
Women are loving
Women are strong
Women are rulers
Women like, women like, women like
Women like gossip
Women like to drink wine
Women like being drama queens
Women like make-up
Women are, women are, women are,
Women are friendly
Women are kind
Women are sexy
Women love cuddly things
Women love men
Women love sweets
Women are sweet
Women can cook
Women love romantic meals
Women love sweet roses
Women love to relax
Women are sensitive
And women do not care what people say
They just want to be.

Tashika Warburton (13)
Skinners' Company's School for Girls (Lower)

Love!

I love you, I love you,
Tell me if you love me.
If you don't, then don't tell me,
If you do, then come and be with me,
And be my love
Forever and ever!

Fatos Evre (13)
Skinners' Company's School for Girls (Lower)

Great Minds

Great minds . . .
Great minds . . .
Great minds all think alike
Like my mum
She gives me life when I need it
She helps me and gives me hope
When I am falling down Hell's deep, dark pit
She is there as a shining rope.

Great minds . . .
Great minds . . .
Great minds all think alike
We are bonded for as long as time stands
We are together always inside
And although Fate is not in my hands
With her my heart always resides.

Great minds
Great minds.

Aminata Fofana (13)
Skinners' Company's School for Girls (Lower)

Famous People

Famous people buy expensive cars
They don't even drive them, they have chauffeurs.
Famous people have lots of money
But yet they don't spend 1p to save a bunny.

Famous people with their big houses,
But I bet some of them have mouses.
Famous people make me sad,
I'm lucky that I ain't gone mad.

Leyla Sokucu (11)
Skinners' Company's School for Girls (Lower)

Great Minds

Great minds . . .
Great minds . . .
What is a great mind?
Is it when you love people?
Think great
A great mind is.

Great minds
Show us great things
Helps us get through life with faith.

Great minds
Show us how great life is.

Great minds . . .
Great minds . . .
Like my best friend and I
We have bonded for as long as time stands
Together and always
Great minds . . .

Niesha Baptiste (13)
Skinners' Company's School for Girls (Lower)

Great Minds

Great minds think alike
At midnight they strike
Like a great white shark
That lurks through the dark.
Great minds think the same,
Through glory and through fame,
The minds think the same.

Victoria Ault (12)
Skinners' Company's School for Girls (Lower)

My Sweet

Round and creamy,
Sour but yummy,
As it's on my tongue, it crackles and snaps,
It smells like strawberry
It feels so smooth but is really hard!
It's red and tasty just like a sweet jam tart,
There's a huge, blue bubblegum inside,
It's double the taste of the sweet itself,
Though it's really delicious and good to eat,
So what more do you want than a creamy,
Round, smooth, tasty, juicy,
Sour and yummy sweet?

Derya Yesilyurt (11)
Skinners' Company's School for Girls (Lower)

Who Is She?

Who is she?
What does she do?
She is different from me and you,
She is powerful and blessed,
Everyone knows she is different from the rest,
Some think she's talented, some think she's talentless
But I think she's the best.
Who is she?
What does she do?
Her name is JK Rowling!
And she writes for me and you!

Laila Hadjimi (11)
Skinners' Company's School for Girls (Lower)

Love Is

Love is you and love is me
Love is a prison and love is free
Love what's there when you're away
Away from me
Love is.
Love is strange and love is everlasting
Love is walking with paint-stained hands
Love is a pink nightdress still slightly worn
Love is.
Love is white panties lying all forlorn
Love is when you have to leave at dawn
Love is forever and love is what happens when
The music stops,
Love is.
Love is the presents in Christmas shops
Love is when you're feeling 'Top of the Pops'
Love is when you don't turn out the light
Love is.

Prisciela Kwatiah (13)
Skinners' Company's School for Girls (Lower)

Great Minds

Great minds are caring
Great minds are bold
Great minds are complicated
Great minds are careful
Like my mum
Great minds are smart
Like me
Great minds are silly
Like my dad.

Joy Akata (13)
Skinners' Company's School for Girls (Lower)

Wise One

If you are walking down a street,
Where thousands of people meet,
Have you ever thought
That one of them couldn't ever be bought?

That they had a brain that had not been found,
A great mind,
That is living normally,
But exceeding out of bounds.

Like maybe a wise, old man,
Who may not know the existence of electrical fans.
Just sitting by the Himalayan mountains,
Trying to invent water fountains.

There's lots of people with different minds
But also with different kinds.
Somewhere alone,
Sitting with an ice cream cone.

Selin Kavlak (13)
Skinners' Company's School for Girls (Lower)

Great Minds

People own great minds
And great minds are people
Everyone is a blessing
That comes from your great mind.
People do things that are encouraged
By great minds,
And great minds are there
So people can use them.

Amandah Simukai (13)
Skinners' Company's School for Girls (Lower)

A Great Mind

A great mind is a growing mind
A great mind is a special mind
A great mind is a righteous mind
A great mind is . . .

A great mind is a creative mind
A great mind will protest for peace
A great mind is forever growing
A great mind is . . .

A great mind is a wonderful mind
A great mind is constantly working
A great mind is our mind
A great mind is . . .

Clio Martin (13)
Skinners' Company's School for Girls (Lower)

Butterflies

I feel butterflies whenever I see you
You make me feel brand new
When I see you I grow weak
Whenever I look at you, I hide and you seek
I'm not your everyday kind of girl
So don't think I'm on sale
Boy you are all I need
Our live is like an unsteady bead
I don't care about the other guys
Because you are the one that gives me butterflies.

Hannah Cowley (13)
Skinners' Company's School for Girls (Lower)

A Great Mind

Roald Dahl, he was a clever fella,
He had a white Jack Russel terrier.
In an apple orchid hut he wrote,
All his children's books, I quote.
This hut was dusty like an old book,
Because he wouldn't let anyone look.
He loved all the spiders in his hut,
He was mad, no one likes spiders, not even my mutt.

Roald Dahl was seventy-four when he died,
Apparently everyone cried.
He accomplished lots in life,
And faced the trouble and the strife.
We thank you for the stories you wrote,
I'll say it again, we thank you, I quote.

Natasha Gane (13)
Skinners' Company's School for Girls (Lower)

Great Minds

Oh thank the great mind
Who made the television
Oh thank the great mind
Who did their revision
Oh thank the great mind
Who invented music
Thank you great mind
For not being *fick*.

Serap Gifci (14)
Skinners' Company's School for Girls (Lower)

Great Minds

A great mind's like someone who prays every day
A great mind's like someone who makes people happy
A great mind's like someone who writes good stories for children.
A great mind is . . .

A great mind's someone who likes people
A great mind's someone who helps people
A great mind's someone who respects people
A great mind's someone who understands.
A great mind is . . .

A great mind's someone who doesn't make wars
A great mind's someone who doesn't kill people
A great mind's someone who doesn't tell lies
A great mind's someone who doesn't trouble people.
A great mind is . . .

Cornelie Dipenge Mayaza (13)
Skinners' Company's School for Girls (Lower)

How Does A Great Mind Work?

What does a great mind think like?
Einstein was a great mind,
He didn't have a problem thinking, I hope.
How does the brain work?
It works like a car,
Sometimes it works, sometimes it fails
But you always tend to live with it.
How does the mouth work?
The mouth works in many ways
'Your mouth is as big as a hippo yawning'
My mother once told me.
Well how does a great mind work?
It works like mine.

Daze Osuide (13)
Skinners' Company's School for Girls (Lower)

Simpsons

The Simpsons are the best,
You just know it . . .
Homer is a doughnut, alcoholic,
He can't deny it . . .
Bart is nothing but trouble,
Everyone knows it . . .
Lisa is an intelligent girl,
Everyone can't get enough of it . . .
Maggie loves her dummy,
We can't hide it . . .
Marge has a blue afro and is a skinny woman
Who doesn't do anything.

Sangeeta Singh (13)
Skinners' Company's School for Girls (Lower)

All About Great Minds

Great minds with the people
Great minds open new things
All of us have great minds
But we don't know we have it within.
People have changed our revolutions
With their brilliant inventions that
Their great minds constructed,
And if you want to find
Your very own great mind,
All you have to do is look inside.

Lucy Stephens (11)
Skinners' Company's School for Girls (Lower)

The Things Parents Say!

Belinda, Belinda the bell is ringing
Belinda, Belinda stop the giggling
Belinda, Belinda you make me gag
Belinda, Belinda sweep the room
Belinda, Belinda use a broom
Belinda, Belinda stop frowning
Belinda, Belinda you make me sad
Belinda, Belinda I'm not in a mood
Belinda, Belinda stop yelling
Belinda, Belinda wash the dishes
Belinda, Belinda where are my wishes?
Belinda, Belinda give me some kisses.

Belinda Sarkodie (13)
St Martin-in-the-Fields High School for Girls

My Daily Do

Time to get up
Brush your hair up
Go wake your sister
Go make your bed up
Eat your crumpets
Don't watch the TV
Now go brush your teeth
Now pack your bag up
Time is moving on
Just don't be late love.

Now uniform off!
So do your homework.
Then eat your dinner,
Then have your shower,
Then turn the lights out
Now just go to bed.

Isha Blake (11)
St Martin-in-the-Fields High School for Girls

My Puppy

The colour of my animal is white with black spots,
It has sharp teeth like a nail and has glittery diamond eyes.
It moves like the wind with its four legs,
It's soft and furry like a teddy bear
It lives in a home with me and it loves me.

Alexandra Chan (13)
St Martin-in-the-Fields High School for Girls

Things Parents Say

Tidy your room,
Fix your hair,
You're late for school,
Why are you here?

Shouting and screaming,
Everyday,
They're my parents,
And they're here to stay.

Off your TV
Do your chores
Do your work,
And here's some more.

Screeching and shouting,
All the time,
They're my parents,
Mine all mine.

Go to bed,
It's getting late,
Don't get me angry,
That's something I'd hate.

Moriam Kolapo (11)
St Martin-in-the-Fields High School for Girls

What My Parents Say To Me

Clean your bedroom,
Make my tea,
Can you go to the shop for me?
Do your homework,
Finish your food,
Go away I'm not in the mood.
Act like a lady,
That skirt's too short.
If you lie to me you're gonna get caught.
Clean your trainers,
Wash the dishes,
Go upstairs and feed the fish.
Wait until your mum comes home,
Tina, I don't want to hear you moan.
That's what my parents say to me make me
Want to jump and scream.

Justina Smith (13)
St Martin-in-the-Fields High School for Girls

Lion's Life

Lie around all day, furry lion now see its prey.
My light brown lion with razor claws, you camouflage with open jaws.
Waiting until your prey's off guard, to gather your strength and
Charge, charge, charge.
King of the jungle proud of your throne
Sly like a snake
You seize your chance.
'Food, food,' the cubs cheerfully say
'We're having a feast, hooray, hooray!'

Latoyah Henry (13)
St Martin-in-the-Fields High School for Girls

What My Parents Say!

Tidy Up
Turn that off
Clean the house
And go to your room
And will it hurt you to
Clean it up?
Turn that on
Be nice
Look at the time
You'd better be off
You're gonna be late
Hurry up, what
Didn't you hear me?
Hurry up!

Remi Oshibanjo
St Martin-in-the-Fields High School for Girls

My Mother!

Chore dodger
Tea guzzler
TV watcher
Food gobbler
Horrible shouter

Tidy upper
Demands a cuppa
Money earner
Time stealer

> *My mother!*

Monique Hector (11)
St Martin-in-the-Fields High School for Girls

Think

It lives in India, hunted in the forest
Its skin as soft as a newborn puppy's
Its eyes are rubies trapped in a black hole
Its tail swinging back and forth, back and forth
It pads the ground like a human patting down soil
Its belly rumbles like a lion protecting his territory
He prowls the forest for food, a king in his palace
Like a hunter gatherer, it spots its victim
He's gone like a child playing hide-and-seek, he hides in the grass
Out of nowhere it pounces, an eagle flying down on its prey
It eats like a beggar given a feast
From behind him a crunching sound comes
Bang!
The forest is empty
The forest is silent
A man walks through wearing a tiger skin coat
A look behind might have saved him
But truth be told the man shouldn't have done it.

Think before you act.

Bethan Chaplin Dewey (11)
St Martin-in-the-Fields High School for Girls

Snake, Snake

Snake, snake, you make me shake
Snake, snake, you make the earth quake.

Snake, snake, I like the way you rattle and shake
Snake, snake, could you be my mate?

Snake, snake, make me a cake
Snake, snake, you are such a big fake.

Sapphire Johnson (13)
St Martin-in-the-Fields High School for Girls

Chores

My parents always have things for me to do
Whether it's going to the shop or shining my shoes
There is never a chore that hasn't been done
So the person to do them, that is me, I'm the one.
Sometimes they try to brighten my day,
I can vacuum the carpet,
But I must do it their way
Then sometimes they can be really fun,
Well, that is only after my chores are done.

Whitney Warren (11)
St Martin-in-the-Fields High School for Girls

My Dog

My dog has got hazel-brown hair,
I look at her and say, 'Come here.'
She's big, cuddly, smooth and soft,
She likes to chase a big, big moth.
She moves like the wind with her tiny little legs
She likes to chew on all the pegs.

Krista Gardier (13)
St Martin-in-the-Fields High School for Girls

Things Parents Say

Eat fruit and veg, clear up the dishes,
Homework, bed, do as I said.
So annoyed, got to avoid the rules of my parents.
TV off. Don't play with my cloth,
Clear up your room, do it soon,
But right now, get to bed,
Do you not hear? Do as I said.

Marian Twenefoo (11)
St Martin-in-the-Fields High School for Girls

The Eye Of The Tiger

Charging at a skilful pace the razor-sharp predator
moves with high and mighty grace.
Its prey, the reddish, bony, bloody, meat of any creature.
Its skin as smooth as a baby's bottom, orange like a tangerine,
and as black as the night.
Its two small, round pebbles staring and staring.
Its pointed cones twitching and twitching as it listens for movement.
Its small round caves itching and itching as it smells its prey.
Then he has it, the razor-sharp predator, has his dinner at last.

Rachael Francis (11)
St Martin-in-the-Fields High School for Girls

There's Always Someone Out There

Every day drags on and on,
There I sit all by myself,
No one helps me as I pray
What shall I do alone all day?

My heart is never full of joy
For no one comes to me,
I look at people laughing and playing,
As I sit there all day, dreaming.

I sit in my enchanted garden,
As the breeze blows through my black silky hair,
Looking at the deep blue sky, so high,
Sooner or later the world will go by.

Soon I discover, that there was no reason to be so glum
For I had met a friendly chum,
She was great and together we were the best,
I know and hope no one will try to put that to the test!

Ayesha Begum (13)
St Martin-in-the-Fields High School for Girls

I've Had Enough!

Tidy your room,
Do your chores,
Pick up your clothes,
I've had enough.

Turn off the TV
Turn down the music,
Come off the computer,
I've had enough.

Get up,
Go to bed,
Turn off the light,
I've had enough.

These are the things my mum would say,
These are the things she said today,
And now she's saying, pick up your stuff,
Oh what's that Mum, you've had enough!

Laela Henley-Rowe (11)
St Martin-in-the-Fields High School for Girls

Camping

C limbing rocks and hard-barked trees,
A nimals biting your knobbly knees,
M oonlit nights in the scary woods,
P eople frightened,
 I nvestigating items,
N ewborn animals when they play,
G oing camping is the fun way.

Adebimpe Eshilokun (11)
St Martin-in-the-Fields High School for Girls

The Dolphin

Leaping and gliding through the blue seawater,
While the bright yellow sun glistens among the calmness.
Its silky and smooth grey body shows that it is a very delicate
                                        and loving mammal.
Eating lots of small fish on the way as it travels through the Pacific,
Warming everything with its touch.
With its small fins and smooth tail nobody can hate this
                                        wonderful creature!

Elizabeth Lancaster (11)
St Martin-in-the-Fields High School for Girls

What Parents Say!

'Do your homework
Go to bed
Where have you been?
It's half-past ten!

Wash the plates
Hoover the floor
Tidy your room
Don't slam that door.

Clean the table
Don't say why?
Clean the bath
And don't be sly.'

'But Mum that is so unfair
Why do I have to do chores all day?'
'Well, darling what should I do
Because that's what parents say.'

Dorcas Oke (11)
St Martin-in-the-Fields High School for Girls

To Be In Love

To be in love is like life itself,
It's complicated and hard to get through it.
You get butterflies every time you see his face,
And pray for the day when you're close to him.
To be in love is a risk
You'll do anything to see him.
When you look into his eyes, you feel like you're drowning,
In a big puddle of water swimming to see his face again.

To be in love, is a beautiful thing,
You feel special when you're around him,
You want to grow old with him,
And to be with him forever.

He is the only one you think about,
You stare at his beautiful face glowing in the room,
And panic when he walks towards you.
Your heart starts to race and you start to sweat.
You wish that he picks you up and holds you in his arms
                                        and never lets go.

Maybe it's not love, you don't know what to think
When you're in love.

Cecilia Omotoso (12)
St Martin-in-the-Fields High School for Girls

Nanny Nanny

Nanny, Nanny you're like honey
I love the way you care.
When you wear your hair you look like a golden pear.
Your flat is always smiling,
When I go in I always feel like shining,
I love the way you cook and share.

Crystal Francis (13)
St Martin-in-the-Fields High School for Girls

The Side Of Heaven

Just this side of Heaven is
A place called Rainbow Bridge
Where does an especially close pet go?
To the place called Rainbow bridge.
What is this place like?
There are meadows and hills.
For special friends, pets.
For running and playing,
With plenty of food, water and sunshine,
Warm and comfortable.
That is the place just this side of Heaven.
Rainbow Bridge.

Rani Laungani (13)
St Martin-in-the-Fields High School for Girls

What My Mum Says To Me

'Get up and wash the dishes,
Sweep the floor,
And feed the fish.

Tidy your room
Turn off the TV,
Help your sister pack away the PC.

Turn down the music
Tell your friends to leave,
Go in the garden and pick up all the leaves.

Go to bed
And come off
The phone
Just you wait
Until your
Dad comes home!'

Markela Mitchell-Welch (13)
St Martin-in-the-Fields High School for Girls

Rainbow

Red,
    Yellow,
        Green,
            Purple,
                Orange,
                    Blue,

All beautiful colours shining brightly
Rain and sun brings the rainbow so clearly
Gives you a very fresh and sweet smell
La, la, la, be, be, be! Birds are singing
The rain teeming down like a beam from a sky
Brings you brightness and happy thoughts.

Kedeesha Morrison-Richards (11)
St Martin-in-the-Fields High School for Girls

Sadness Of Love

I stand in the corner,
And stare with horror!

I stare through the window,
And soon I'll be a widow.

My husband is in pain,
I'm standing in the rain.

I'm waiting for the news,
He's badly bruised.

I wonder - will he survive?
If he doesn't I'll surely die.

I hold my bag tightly in my arms,
But will he ever return?

Harriet Leyden (12)
St Martin-in-the-Fields High School for Girls

Parents Rap

Read your book
Don't give me that look!
Tidy your room
And sweep with the broom!

Do this, do that
Don't wear that hat!
I'm telling your dad,

Where have you been?
You pre-teen!
Do your chores!
Clean the dog's paws!
Time for dinner!
Go help Linda!

Lights out!
And clean the dog's snout!

Tolani Adekoya (12)
St Martin-in-the-Fields High School for Girls

Friendship

F riendship with your family
R eally with your friends
I n the school or at your home
E verywhere there's friends
N o one stops
D aring just
S hare's a happy time
H aving friends
I t's lots of fun
P lay with them 'til nine.

Tia-Victoria Brown (11)
St Martin-in-the-Fields High School for Girls

Bad Girls

The boys in their beds,
Are afraid to come out,
It's winter and it's dark,
And the bad girls are about.

The grannies with their trolleys,
Are rushing along.
The bad girls are scary,
And what they're doing is wrong.

The kids are at the park,
They stop all their play,
Rush to their mothers,
Or the girls will make them pay.

No one is out after nine o'clock,
Because that's the time you're not secure.
The doors and windows are locked and barred,
The girls rob the rich, but not the poor.

At home the girls sleep through the day,
They are snoring like pigs
The citizens decide to play a trick,
By making a giant quite big.

The girls wake up
They have a fright,
They scream and shout,
And give in without a fight.

The girls are good now,
But for the best start,
No giant can change them,
They need a new heart!

Mercy Weidenmüller (11)
St Martin-in-the-Fields High School for Girls

Do It!

Wake up, wake up,
You'll be late for school
Wake up! Wake up!
Cleaning is a rule.

Have you done your homework?
Have you cleaned the house?
Have you brushed your teeth yet?
Have you caught that mouse?

Wake up, wake up,
You'll be late for school
Wake up! Wake up!
Cleaning is a rule.

Get off that computer,
Go and take a bath
What is so funny?
Don't stay and have a laugh.

Wake up, wake up,
You'll be late for school,
Wake up! Wake up!
Cleaning is a rule.

Go and wash the dog now,
Go and wash your hair,
Do the washing up now
I really do not care!

Natalie Aboaku (12)
St Martin-in-the-Fields High School for Girls

What Parents Always Say!

Don't you think it's annoying,
When parents always say.

Tidy your room!
Wake up now!

It always ruins my day

Hurry up or you'll be late!
Is another one they may say.

If I ask my mum for money,
She'll tell me to ask my dad.
And when I ask my dad,
He'll send me away sad.

Then the next minute it's a whole different story
They treat me, with sooo much glory.

Lauren Rugless (11)
St Martin-in-the-Fields High School for Girls

My Little Puppy

My little puppy is cutie and bright
His name is Fluffy and he's brown and white
He lives in my house, just like me
He uses his paws, like my feet
He's soft and smooth and I love him to bits
So we'll never separate for billions of years.

Isabel Crankson (11)
St Martin-in-the-Fields High School for Girls

Things Parents Say

Turn it down,
Turn it up,
Do the washing up,
Do your homework,
Don't stay out too late,
Here's some money,
Don't spend it all at once,
Turn the TV off,
Turn the TV on,
Tell your friends to come in,
It's getting a bit chilly out,
Go out and leave me in peace,
I'm going out,
Don't have too much fun,
And most of all *don't make a mess!*

Samantha Smyth (11)
St Martin-in-the-Fields High School for Girls

Koala

Koala so high in the sky,
Koala so furry and soft,
He climbs this way so high in the sky,
Koala so furry and soft.

Big nose, big claws, big ears, for hearing
Up in the tree too high for me, big ears for hearing.

He's grey and black, never would attack
He's so cute,
Always mute,
Gosh he's just so cute,
Gosh and he's so mute.

Ebony Smith-Fyffe (11)
St Martin-in-the-Fields High School for Girls

Great Writers Of The World

They sit in their studies, all tidy and neat,
Thoroughly sucking a hard boiled sweet.
Thinking up stories to make children laugh,
About witches, tin men and a yellow brick path.

Oh golly, oh gosh, what will happen next?
Will they be happy or will they be vexed?

Will Lord Sauron rule Middle Earth?
Who will reach VFD Headquarters first?

Oh writers of the world, please don't stop there!
Or all us children will fall into despair.

Mia Roberts (12)
St Martin-in-the-Fields High School for Girls

What Parents Say

Shut up, be quiet,
Can't they go away,
That's how I feel when they're moaning away
They get on my nerves
I want to shout and scream.

Just leave me alone and don't bother me
I'm doing my homework,
That's what I'll tell them
They'll probably come back,
With a frown, not a grin.

Jodeci Rowe-Matthews (11)
St Martin-in-the-Fields High School for Girls

A Garden Full Of Love

Love is like a flower
You have to tend it, feed it, grow it, help it,
If you don't, the flower will die, love will die.

The leaves are like the different parts of love
The kindness, the happiness, the trust.
One may fall and the flower won't be the same.

Like love, the flower is rooted down,
Not breaking up, not dying
It flourishes and makes everything sunny
Even on days that have things that are not quite right
Love heals that, love makes the day bright.

People like love, people like flowers,
But there's one thing flowers don't have
Unlike plants, love can live forever
In your mind, in the air and in your heart.

Rosanna Neophytou (13)
The Grey Coat Hospital

What Is An Angelfish?

What is an angelfish?
Its tail is as thin as a pin,
Its skin scaly but sleek,
It's like a balloon flowing through the air.
Its eyes piercing and black, as black as coal,
In the sea it looks for food,
On the seabeds it looks like rocks,
Fins moving up and down it, looking like waves,
In the deep blue sea it becomes an enemy's prey,
Swimming, it becomes an angel drifting up to Heaven
Grace swims with it.

Sophie Mitchell (11)
The Grey Coat Hospital

The Hero (Or Should It Be The Zero?)

I'm excellent at English
I'm amazing at maths
I'm very good at science
And I'm top of my history class.

I'm like an atlas in geography
Like an artist in DT
I'm an actor in my drama lessons
I could be on TV.

I'm brilliant at swimming
I can score a great goal
I am very fast when running
And can dig like a mole.

At school I'm very popular
I'm known as a hero
But compared to my baby sister
I'm a *big fat zero!*

Gjeta Gjyshinca (11)
The Grey Coat Hospital

The Heat

My alarm clock rings
I have to wake
To see the early morning break.

The birds are chirping,
The sky *is getting lighter,*
The dull clouds are dissolving,
The day is approaching,
Approaching, approaching.

The climate is rising,
Heat as hot as lava,
A burning stick in the fire,
No soul's desire.

Kai Noel-Lalgie (11)
The Grey Coat Hospital

Great Mind To Show!

'Great mind'.

A great mind is a special gift,
A great mind is an intelligent gift.
Great minds, will think alike
Great minds always help us to try
A great mind makes us make the right decision
'Great mind'.

Great minds help us to be what we want to be.
Great minds help us to be treated right.
Great minds will give us a chance to understand
A great mind is a wonderful piece of life.
Great minds is what we are and what we truly need.

'Great mind'.

A great mind is when you give someone a second chance.
Great minds help us to show great interest.
A great mind helps us to gain more knowledge
In our everyday life.

Stephanie Baynes (13)
The Grey Coat Hospital

What Is A Giraffe?

Its face is like a smooth soft cloth,
Its neck is longer than a long log,
Its eyes are like fluffy peaches,
Its mouth is like a washing machine,
Its legs are hard, long sticks,
Its golden hairs are as thin as straws,
Its feet are like horse shoes,
Its skin is like a patchwork quilt.

Its tongue is long like a frog's
Its ears are like two satellite dishes.
Height sways with it.

Lolade Akande (11)
The Grey Coat Hospital

Sunflower

The falling rain, the shining sun,
The fields where ochre sunflowers run.
Some seeds fall out, and then they grow
While their parents die and go.
The chain goes on, again, again,
It goes on through sun and rain.
Like love it is forever lasting
Even when the time is passing.

Rachel Dargavel-Leafe (13)
The Grey Coat Hospital

I Miss You

I think about you often,
I talk about you too.
I have such precious memories,
I wish I still had you.

We're not really separate,
We're like two vines entwined.
I miss you more than anything,
I wish I could turn back time.

You'll never see me married,
Get my licence or my car.
No more precious memories,
Because you are so far.

A year's gone by now,
The pain is still the same.
I've dried my tears, got no more fears,
But I'll never forget your name.

The day you went away
My heart broke in two.
Now you're gone, I just wanna say,
I miss you.

Emma Lawler (13)
The Grey Coat Hospital

A Poem To Our Slavers

You drag us around like we are dirt.
You treat us like we are lower than you.
You hate us, but what have we done to you?

You whip us.
You beat us.
You rape us.
You spit on us.

Is this the world that we want to live in?
A place where people live in fear of death?
In fear or pain?

Why the hatred?
Why the pain?
Why the suffering?
Why the deaths?

Who are we?

Slaves.

Crispina Wilson-Jones (13)
The Grey Coat Hospital

What Is A Teacher?

Someone who helps you,
Someone who cares for you,
Someone who you may see everyday,
Someone you may hate, someone you may like,
They're there to help you if you like,
So help them truly, when you listen,
Keep your business outside their rooms,
And they'll probably treat you as good as new,
That's all for now,
So next time you enter the room, remember this poem.

Jennifer Oppong-Nyantakyi (11)
The Grey Coat Hospital

Alone

Alone I shine,
Alone I am beautiful
When you can no longer see me, you feel no loss
For something better has come along.

I stick by your side
By your every trouble
Through all your pain and doubt.
But you have already forgotten I even exist.

Like a useless statue you shut me away
Basking in her deathly glow.
But one day she will stop
And I will still be there, alone.

I am like the moon,
Cold and alone.
Taken for granted until you need me
That's what I am.
A piece of background furniture,
Cold and alone in my own little world.

One day like a solar eclipse
I will block out the light from the sun.

And on that day you will finally realise
That I am actually someone.

Gemma Newlands (13)
The Grey Coat Hospital

Lion

Its mane gift of beauty
Its tail, a dangerous piece of string
The king of the jungle he will always be
The body is a masculine piece of art
Its eyes twinkled in the moonlight
Death walks with it.

Jessica Thomas (11)
The Grey Coat Hospital

A Broken Heart

A broken heart is an endless pain,
A flight of depression seeps through the veins,
The heart pumps a continuous beat,
Provoking the eyes to water and weep.

A broken heart is a time of anger,
Eyes full of hatred that blaze on fire,
A gust of sorrow blows upon the face of despair,
Whose fury swiftly disperses in the air.

A broken heart delivers a burden of tears,
The skin shivers with anxiety and fear,
An attempt to escape and travel beyond,
Is running an everlasting marathon.

A broken heart is a fearful dream,
Consternation transforms into cries and screams,
In some hour or so the eyes will awaken,
To realise their happiness has not been taken.

Chloe Powell (13)
The Grey Coat Hospital

What Is A Panther?

Its head is like the sky at night,
With glittering stars for eyes
Its body blends with darkness,
As the panther walks around suspiciously
Like a sniper ready to attack.

The panther is sly, waits for any prey,
They're not safe in a jungle,
For every corner lurks a predator -
A panther.

Nina Dougan (11)
The Grey Coat Hospital

What Is A Cat?

Its head, small and round, with piercing eyes that watch you,
Its body, soft and warm like a bed of feathers
Its face, shows little expression, just like a doll.
Its ears, small and pointy like party hats,
Its nose, small and never moves, like a radar picking up the scent.
He purrs, his kingdom dances with joy,
As he cries, the people cry too,
He wanders away, we miss him,
He rolls on his back, dirt covers him like a blanket.
Then he moves and the silence walks with him.

Georgia Reid-Hamilton (12)
The Grey Coat Hospital

Love Is A Dice

We're not really separate,
We're like a dice,
We take many chances,
But we take them together.

Sometimes we're lucky,
Sometimes we're not,
But as long as we're together,
Lucky or not, we really love each other.

Every part of us might be different,
But we're still the same,
We will never break,
We are strong.

Love binds us together,
Love breaks us apart,
It might fade,
But as long as we're in love, it won't.

So let's stay together.

Amna Burzic (13)
The Grey Coat Hospital

What Is A Bird?

Its head is like an egg,
Its eyes, wide and round,
Its body is like a shape, that has never been discovered.
Its outer body is furry and has features
Its feet are as pink as a pig.

It flies with its wings open and its legs tucked in,
It flies with air blowing on its features till it gets to its destination.

And when it opens its mouth to call its friends,
It twitters and sounds amazing.

Andrea Olayiwola (12)
The Grey Coat Hospital

Spellbound

Blood, blood everywhere,
Now drop in mortal's hair.

In the cauldron boil and bake,
I will put a poisoned snake.
Now to add a bit of flavour,
I will put a dead man's tongue to savour.

Blood, blood everywhere,
Now drop in mortal's hair.

In the cauldron I will put,
A bit of one large mortal's foot.
Add a toe, add a finger,
To make the cats want to linger.

Blood, blood everywhere,
Now drop in mortal's hair.

In goes an eye of rat,
In goes a tail of cat.
Now to finish this evil spell,
I will put a dead snail's shell!

Natasha Savovic (11)
The Grey Coat Hospital

Save The Koala

S mall snub nose,
A ustralia is their home.
V enturing out in the wild,
E ndangered because of us.

T heir habitat is running out fast
H ear their bellowing cries,
E ucalyptus leaves their source of food.

K illed for their fur a long time ago,
O f all the things to be sorted out, koalas should come first.
A lot of eucalyptus leaves they eat in one day
L ovely, cute animals
A ll we have to do is stop cutting their trees down.

F ur is waterproof when the rain falls,
R unning from bush fires
O ur fault, they're nearly gone
M y favourite animal is nearly extinct.

E xtinction will come next,
X -rays into the future are not possible
T oo upsetting to see them go,
I and you are to blame
N o animals like them on the whole planet,
C ould you just think of them for one minute?
T he rule not to kill koalas is not helping,
I n the eucalyptus leaves they hide,
O n their own or in big groups,
N ow try and save the koalas from extinction.

Bethany Hitchcock (11)
The Grey Coat Hospital

I Would Like To . . .

I would like to see through people's minds,
To make sure they are kind.
I would like to fly to Heaven
To visit all my friends.

During the night, breathe in the air,
I would like to catch the star.
During the day, enjoy my time,
I would like to visit the clouds.

I would like to be a millionaire,
To help all the people out.
I would like to visit my imagination,
To try and make them real.

From the north to the south,
I would like to travel by my wings,
Up in the sky, ask the bird,
Where is your house?

I would like to know the colour of the wind,
Is it black, pink or green?
I would like to know the taste of the air,
Is it chocolate, strawberry or nothing?

I would like to travel all around the world,
To investigate all the mysteries.
I would like to go deeply into the sea,
To search for Nemo the fish.

Verna Gao (11)
The Grey Coat Hospital

We Are Never Really Apart

We're not really ever apart
We are two peas in a pod
Can be pushed apart by others
But eventually end up on
The same plate together.

I make you smile
You make me laugh.

We entwine ourselves
Around each other but
With every twist, more and more care,
Hope, joy, love and laughter is added.

You would leave but slowly and swiftly
You would return to me
Our hearts are two but beat as one.

We are like wrinkles
Can't see them at first
But slowly after time
We will shine out as our love grows.

Ashley Lawson-Jacobs (13)
The Grey Coat Hospital

What Is A Rabbit?

What is a rabbit?
Its head, a furry ball.
Its ears, a pair of long pronged knives,
Its body is like the rain, pitter-pattering really fast,
Its tail, a ball of fluff,
Its tiny claws are like pointed scissors,
On the ground - it is jumping around,
Jumping, it becomes a bouncy ball,
Eating on the grass, it chews like a human chewing bubblegum.
The happiness hops with it.

Rabia Alibaig (11)
The Grey Coat Hospital

Black Beauty

My beauty gallops in the sun,
He glistens and sparkles,
He rolls around in the mud
He's turned out for four hours.

He's brought back to the stable
That's when he's tacked up
Then he's ready for Handy Pony
Or maybe even dressage.

He's brought out on the yard,
Led out to the forecourt,
The rider then jumps on,
And warms up round the farm.

We get back to the forecourt,
He's led into the menage,
He gallops from the starting line,
And then wins first place.

My pony's led back on the yard
He's nervous with a chill,
'I wonder what prize I've won,'
It will just be brill.

Perri O'Connor (11)
The Grey Coat Hospital

What Is A Leopard?

What is a leopard?
Its fur as fine as silk,
Its body so streamlined,
Its ears so sharp at even the slightest noise,
On the ground it is in motion,
Approaching its prey, invisible to the eye,
Its eye glittering in the sun,
Disaster walks with it.

Hope McFarlane-Edmond (11)
The Grey Coat Hospital

I Should Like . . .

I should like to touch the stars,
Reach up tall and stand on Mars,
Stand on the clouds, watch the planes,
Grow myself a lion's mane.

> I should like to run a house,
> Then transform myself into a mouse.
> Then I'll fly like an eagle,
> Move up and down with my Beagle.

I should like to touch the rain,
Stop all the snow and the pain.
For there to be light in people's lives
Then there should be no more strife.

> I should like to see peace on Earth,
> Walk up and down through my church.
> Thanking God for all I have had,
> And thinking and praying for people who are sad.

Dianne Lutalo (11)
The Grey Coat Hospital

I Would Like To . . .

I would like to dive into the deep blue ocean,
And hear the fish roam freely.
I would like to taste the fluffy white clouds in the
Beautiful morning sky.
I would like to smell the blaze of the burning sun.
I would like to see the voice of someone talking to me.
I would like to hold the wind's hand as it breezes through
The bushes catching joy and wonder as it goes by!

Takyiwa Danso (11)
The Grey Coat Hospital

I Would Like . . .

I would like to be able to smell the sky and taste the clouds,
Touch the birds while they are singing,
On a hot summer's morning.

I would like to touch a star, smell a star, taste a star
And see the glow of a star.

I would like to go out to sea go down under the water
Touch and smell the colourful fish
Taste the beautiful shells and to be able to feel the smooth water
on my skin.

I would like to hear the Niagara Falls,
See the trickles of chocolate on the rocks,
Feel the gushes of chocolate on my face.

Lotty Lovejoy-Crump (11)
The Grey Coat Hospital

The Sun

I heat things up like a cooker
To the world I am an onlooker.

My body is golden and tanned,
I have a likeness to a stretched out hand.

I look like a lion's mane
In the rush hour I drive people insane.

I wear a cloak of orange and yellow,
I make people's moods lovely and mellow.

Seeping and creeping through houses and towns,
I never fail to prevent a frown.

I light up the sky like a lamp,
After rain has fallen I cure the damp.

Georgia Tully (11)
The Grey Coat Hospital

What Is A Cat?

Its head, just like a human's.
Its ears as pointy as the spikes on a fence.
Its chest, hardly visible except for the fur around it.
Its body, like a jacket potato with two arms, two legs,
A tail and a head poking out.
Its paws, like a computer print,
Its tail, like a snake.
Its two yellow eyes with a black diamond in the centre.
Its nose a circle with two holes punched in, like ears
Which have just been pierced.
Its mouth hidden behind bushy whiskers,
When cats walk, they walk in proud.
When cats lie down, they lie down proud.
When it's been raining on the mud,
And when a cat goes walking,
Mud walks with it.

Ophelia Gibson Best (11)
The Grey Coat Hospital

Love

Though my journey takes me far,
Our love will bind us forever,
So evermore in mind and soul,
We'll always be together.

I know I'm going far away,
Through the temptations of this world,
But my heart will forever be yours,
So never lead it astray.

So again I say I love you
For you can never say it more
In this world of toil and fear,
You need someone to care for.

Katy Brock (13)
The Grey Coat Hospital

What Is A Baby Cheetah?

Its face, as innocent as a young baby.
Its ears, as pointy as a witch's nose.
Its tear marks, as sorrowful as a lonely widow.
Its teeth, as sharp as a sword waiting to rip into your skin.
Its claws, as long as a blade, waiting to slash out and dig into you.
When running, it is like a hurricane swooping around the Earth.
When catching prey, it is like war, killing one and then the next.
When hiding, it is like a camouflaged frog, not hiding from attackers,
                                            but going to attack.
When sleeping, its ears are still open like an elephant,
Never missing one single sound.
    Fearfulness walks with it.

Zoë Zvimba (11)
The Grey Coat Hospital

What Is A Snake?

It's a slithering snake that slithers through light and dark,
Its tongue comes in and out like a piece of string hanging
                                        from its mouth,
It sends a shiver down everybody's spine
Fear slithers with it!

On the ground it lays there waiting,
The ground seems to be the snake's favourite place,
Approaching on the ground, its colours glitter in the sun,
Fear slithers with it!

Lying on the grass the snake becomes a snake in peace,
Slithering it becomes a twig moving all around the grass,
Fear slithers with it!

Olivia White (11)
The Grey Coat Hospital

As I Wandered Through The Fields

I know a place where there are
Beautiful big sunflowers
The scented smell will last for hours.
On the grasslands
Poppies flutter and flow
While in the bright sky
The wind starts to blow.
Under the tall tree
There sleeps a delightful princess
Her long fair hair
Matches her long fair dress.
The chilly breeze,
Is making her numb
But something evil and wicked
This way will come . . .

Olamide Subair (11)
The Grey Coat Hospital

What Is A Fox?

What is a fox?
Its fur, red as blood,
Its ears always pricked and ready,
Its eyes, evil-looking and suspicious,
A sly and cunning creature,
It runs through trees and danger,
Seeking its one destination,
Its teeth sharp as razors,
Claws as lethal as knives,
It pounces, it kills,
Then it returns home,
Wide-eyed and innocent,
With its prey in its mouth,
Death trailing behind it.

Rachel Davies (11)
The Grey Coat Hospital

My Poem

I wish I could hold the stars,
Run as fast as a car.

I wish I could eat the Milky Way
And think of as many words I can say.

Oh do I, do I wish . . .

I wish I could touch the clouds
And *shout* and be so *loud*.

See the Heavens above
So when I die I'll be loved.

Oh do I, do I wish . . .

I wish I could hear the wind blow quiet or loud
Hold the world and see the planet.

Oh do I, do I wish . . .

Betty Crabbe (11)
The Grey Coat Hospital

What Is A Lion?

What is a lion?
Its mane a ball of fire,
Its teeth a razor saw,
Its body like a cloud,
Its eyes quick as lightning,
Over the field it pounces,
Cutting the grass as it ran,
Touching the ground it is camouflaged,
Its deafening roar explodes through Africa,
Pride walks with it.

Casia Dunning (11)
The Grey Coat Hospital

I Should Like

I should like to hear the angels sing
I should like to relax on the wide open channel
I should like to feel the bird's songs
I should like to see the bird's words
I should like to see the future
I should like to hear the forest
I should like to taste the sun
I should like to hear the ocean
I should like to hear the wind blowing,
I should like to see the wind blowing
I should like to feel the breeze of the wind
I should like to feel the music flowing
I should like to float in the sky
I should like to taste the clouds
I should like to see the dark glowing
I should like to see the dark glowing.

Chanielle Abdullie-Stewart (11)
The Grey Coat Hospital

The Midnight Prowler

What is a midnight prowler?
Its eyes, bright like the sun,
Its ears, stick up,
Its tail, furry like himself,
Its nose, wet like the rain,
His scent sudden and quick,
He lands on his feet if he falls,
His miaow so discreet,
He prowls on the rooftops,
Night prowls with him.

Shaquelle Northover-Neita (11)
The Grey Coat Hospital

Running Waters

The river is a dancing fountain, set apart with joy and hope.
It's ready to do harm.
As bright as the day there would be no sound that would let loose
From the tower of happiness.
The cool waves crashing against her joy, clouds filling her
Anger but emptying gladness.
The glistening waterfalls sparkle in the rays of the sun;
She seemed to glisten with the sun in her dazzling imagination.
Voices of spoken joy were from the whistling wind's breeze,
Making her hair sway like the leaves on the branch.
Like spitting rain the frantic bugs ruined the harvest.
The peace that always stood by her would always stay with those
who would catch the light.

Jessica McCarthy (11)
The Grey Coat Hospital

Africa

In the dry warm area of Africa a giraffe so strong, tall and bold,
Was walking by the sunset that was anything but cold.
The red and the yellow like fire shone on the clearing ahead,
And the giraffe started to admire it by swaying and turning his head.

His long graceful neck stretched up to the leafiest tree,
And listened, listened ever so softly.

His tail swinging, swinging with the beat, the beat of the African heart.
And he thought to himself that he and Africa will never be apart.

Catherine Lynch (11)
The Grey Coat Hospital

Winter

White snow drifts through the sky,
The red robins tweet and fly
The holly is sharp as the air
The ashes, love's fire left in the cold
And the king's gift of gold
The story ever told.

Angel's wings through the throng
The candles roaring song
The bells, they chime so bright
The darkness of the night
The chiming bells alight.

Jennifer Hardy (14)
The Grey Coat Hospital

The Colour Of Water

What is the colour of water?
Some put it as blue,
Some put it as clear,
Some put it as green,
But if you take all three water colours,
It seems to be clear.
So what is the colour of water?
Why do we see it as blue?
Why do we see it as clear?
Why do we see it as green?
Is it something to do with our sight?
No!
So what is the colour of water?

Crispina Jac-During (11)
The Grey Coat Hospital

Seeing What The Eyes Cannot

I should like to feel the Earth's atmosphere,
To listen to the silence of the leaves in the trees.
To see the sun's watchful eye
I should like to smell the soft spring waters,
Wade into the bright blue sky,
To taste the sound of worldly laughter.

I should like to spread my wings,
Fly into the sky with nothing more
Than the wind on my back
To soar through the air
Seeing the sound of the seagull's cry
To feel the tear of the sky's distress
And help soothe all pain.

I should like to converse
With the angels of the night
To touch the marshmallow clouds
To watch the taste of melted chocolate
To smell the bubble that lightly falls
And taste the green of every blade of grass.

Shannon Royce (11)
The Grey Coat Hospital

I Should Like . . .

I should like to swim in lava,
Fly like a bird over the rooftops.
I should like to hear the wind sing,
And be the breeze that's singing.
I should like to stand on the sun,
And catch a falling star.
I should like to slide down a rainbow.

   And find . . .

        (. . . a volcano).

Thea Poysden (11)
The Grey Coat Hospital

Empty Schoolyard

The last person leaves,
Rushing from the end of another school day,
Leaving the playground empty,
Apart from me.

I start to walk,
Through the now dark shelter,
Where in the day's schoolbags lie,
And people climb the wooden struts on the wall.

I make my way up the playground,
Past the concrete lines,
Where in the day people run up and down,
Pretending to be aeroplanes.

I walk past the sand dust wall,
With muddy marks that hang like clouds -
Where in the day footballs thud their tune,
And people cry out the score.

I jog past the furrow in the grass,
A scar on green skin,
Where in the day people run,
Shouting and laughing.

And then I start to run,
Putting my jacket in the shelter, I climb on the wooden strutts
on the wall.

Then I run down the concrete lines
Pretending to be an aeroplane.
I kick my muddy football against the sand dust wall
Run across the grass . . .
And wait for tomorrow.

Lettecia Smith (11)
The Grey Coat Hospital

I'd Like To Be A Bird

I should like to be a bird,
And skim the ocean blue.
I would hunt for food in the morning,
And play in the afternoon.

As the rain is pitter-pattering on my foot,
I see birds fly under shelter for safety.
Their feathers are red, green, blue and purple,
But now they look fluffy and ugly.

I want to be a tiger,
And race through the grass.
I would wake up really early in the mornings,
And sleep in the afternoon.

As I watch the TV
I see the tigers run
But they're trying to catch a baby deer
Now they have run after them.

Those are my two best animals
And I like them so much
But maybe I'm just better being, being, being, me!

Pauline Solademi (11)
The Grey Coat Hospital

What Is A Piranha?

Its teeth, a bloody blade,
Its tail flapping deadly,
Its eyes, gawking at its prey,
Its head is a fat lump of chicken,
Its scales moving up and down for hunger,
Destruction swims with it.

Divya Patel (11)
The Grey Coat Hospital

Shadow Of The Night

The stars glisten on a dappled grey night
All is silent and the whole world seems to have fallen into the
         deepest of slumbers,
As if a twinkling fairy has cast on them an enchanted sleep,
From which they have no hope or wish of escaping.

Buy why would they?
The night is not for the good and the kind,
The night is not for the gentle and sweet,
And the night is not for the innocent and true.
The night is for me, but not for you.

The darkness is owned by the shadowed people
For those who sold their souls, or have been shunned by society,
The outcasts, the guilty, the condemned,
Or those who just lost their way . . .

And now wander the winding maze of the moonlit city,
Following the flickering street lamps,
Past forbidden alleys and dingy streets,
And then there is me, who doesn't belong,
Never has and never will even in this world of misfits.

Cruelly destined to wander alone after you,
You who have not seen the night,
Not puzzled its mysteries or feared its darkest corners,
But I will always follow you,
But a moment behind, like your shadow,
I will never leave your side.

Whether you see me or not, I will always be there
Cloaked in the darkness, helpless to my unknown, undying love,
Wherever there is sunshine, there will be darkness,
Wherever there is you, there will be me.

Anna Hobbs (13)
The Grey Coat Hospital

I Should Like To . . .

I should like to . . .
Feel the children's laughter
Echoing through the breeze.
I should like to . . .
Fall asleep in a book's arms,
Drift off into another world,
Let my imagination run wild,
Jump from cloud to cloud,
In the sky so blue,
Free from all troubles that worry.
I should like to . . .
Wake up on a summer's day
And hear the sun chuckling in my ear.
Its rays of power shining on my face,
Making me smile throughout the day.
I should like to . . .
Touch the freezing cold snow,
My hands on the floor making snowballs,
And snowmen with a bobble hat and a carrot nose.
Yes, that's what I should like to do.

Christy Parks (11)
The Grey Coat Hospital

My Poem

I should like to touch the glittering stars,
Hear the mighty waves crashing from side to side.
I should like to smell the fresh green grass,
The sight of the crystal clear sea.
I should like to hear the beautiful sound of the birds singing,
Taste the hot, burning sun.
I would be able to fly to the clouds,
And fly through the lovely fresh air.
The sound of the wind passing by your face.
The raindrops fall on my face.

Kimberley Cooper (11)
The Grey Coat Hospital

The Journey Of Two Friends

Our friendship is like a flower
It starts off with a seed so small,
And yet, just with some TLC, it starts to grow so tall.

Our friendship cannot be perfect.
From time to time, our petals shall wilt,
But because our friendship is so strong,
Things will get better; I know we'll be friends forever.

Our friendship is like an elevator
It starts off very slow,
But with time we get to know each other, our friendship
                                                                    starts to grow.

Our friendship cannot be perfect.
From time to time, the elevator will stop,
But because our friendship is so powerful,
It will only go to the very top.

Our friendship is like a washing machine
It starts off with such little might,
If we add more hope and trust, we'll be sure to win the fight.

Our friendship cannot be perfect.
From time to time, the washing will come to a halt,
But as our friendship is unbreakable,
We'll forever work together like pepper and salt.

Lydia Rose (13)
The Grey Coat Hospital